AMERICA'S NATIONAL PARKS

YOSEMITE
NATIONAL PARK

ADVENTURE, EXPLORE, DISCOVER

STEPHEN FEINSTEIN

MyReportLinks.com Books
an imprint of

Enslow Publishers, Inc.

MyReportLinks.com Books, an imprint of Enslow Publishers, Inc. MyReportLinks® is a registered trademark of Enslow Publishers, Inc.

Library of Congress Cataloging-in-Publication Data

Feinstein, Stephen.
  Yosemite National Park : adventure, explore, discover / Stephen Feinstein.
      p. cm. — (America's national parks)
  Summary: "A virtual tour of Yosemite National Park, with chapters devoted to the history of this region, history of the park, plant and animal life, environmental problems facing the park, and activities in the area"—Provided by publisher.
  Includes bibliographical references and index.
  ISBN-13: 978-1-59845-095-8 (hardcover)
  ISBN-10: 1-59845-095-6 (hardcover)
  1. Yosemite National Park (Calif.)—Juvenile literature. I. Title.
  F868.Y6F437 2009
  979.4'47—dc22
                                    2007039045

Printed in the United States of America

10 9 8 7 6 5 4 3 2 1

To Our Readers:
Through the purchase of this book, you and your library gain access to the Report Links that specifically back up this book.
The Publisher will provide access to the Report Links that back up this book and will keep these Report Links up to date on **www.myreportlinks.com** for five years from the book's first publication date.
We have done our best to make sure all Internet addresses in this book were active and appropriate when we went to press. However, the author and the Publisher have no control over, and assume no liability for, the material available on those Internet sites or on other Web sites they may link to.
The usage of the MyReportLinks.com Books Web site is subject to the terms and conditions stated on the Usage Policy Statement on **www.myreportlinks.com**.
A password may be required to access the Report Links that back up this book. The password is found on the bottom of page 4 of this book.
Any comments or suggestions can be sent by e-mail to comments@myreportlinks.com or to the address on the back cover.

♻ Enslow Publishers, Inc., is committed to printing our books on recycled paper. The paper in every book contains 10% to 30% post-consumer waste (PCW). The cover board on the outside of each book contains 100% PCW. Our goal is to do our part to help young people and the environment too!

Photo Credits: Bryan Swan & Dean Goss, p. 16; C. Madrid French, p. 98; California Travel & Tourism Commission, p. 14; © Corel Corporation, p. 8–9, 19, 86; Courtesy of Kevin Berry, p. 31; Dan Anderson, p. 56; Defenders of Wildlife, p. 21; Discover A Hobby Inc., p. 113; ESPERE-ENC, p. 81; Friends of Yosemite Search and Rescue, p. 109; Library of Congress, p. 63; Michael E. Ritter, p. 82; MyReportLinks.com Books, p. 4; National Geographic Society, p. 74; National Park Service, pp. 38, 42, 69, 103, 104, 105; National Park Service/Enslow Publishers, Inc., p. 5; NPCA, p. 100; Orbitz Away LLC, p. 76; PBS/WGBH Science Unit, p. 36; Restore Hetch Hetchy, p. 65; Shutterstock.com, pp. 1, 3, 6–7, 22–23, 26–27, 33, 41, 44–45, 47, 49, 52–53, 58, 66–67, 72, 78–79, 92, 94, 106, 111, 114–115, and all chapter-opener photos of electronics; Sierra Club John Muir Education Committee, p. 61; Smithsonian National Museum of Natural History, p. 89; United Nations, p. 97; University of Michigan, p. 90; U.S. Department of the Interior, p. 102; U.S. Geological Survey, p. 29; WWF, p. 84; Yosemite Association, p. 24; Yosemitehikes.com, p. 116; Yosemite-National-Park.org, p. 12.

Cover Photos: Shutterstock.com

CONTENTS

MyReportLinks.com Books
Great Books, Great Links, Great for Research!

The Internet sites featured in this book can save you hours of research time. These Internet sites—we call them **"Report Links"**—are constantly changing, but we keep them up to date on our Web site.

When you see this "Approved Web Site" logo, you will know that we are directing you to a great Internet site that will help you with your research.

Give it a try! Type http://www.myreportlinks.com into your browser, click on the series title and enter the password, then click on the book title, and scroll down to the Report Links listed for this book.

The Report Links will bring you to great source documents, photographs, and illustrations. MyReportLinks.com Books save you time, feature Report Links that are kept up to date, and make report writing easier than ever! A complete listing of the Report Links can be found on pages 118–119 at the back of the book.

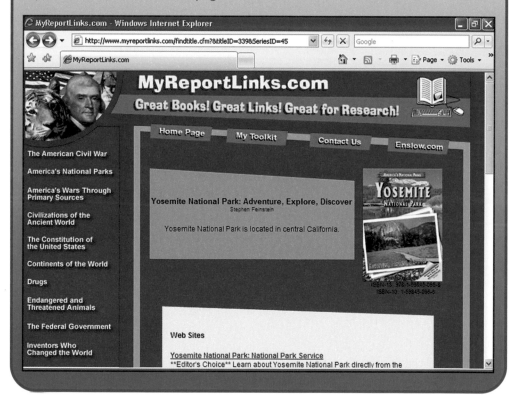

Please see "To Our Readers" on the copyright page for important information about this book, the MyReportLinks.com Web site, and the Report Links that back up this book.

Please enter YOP1682 if asked for a password.

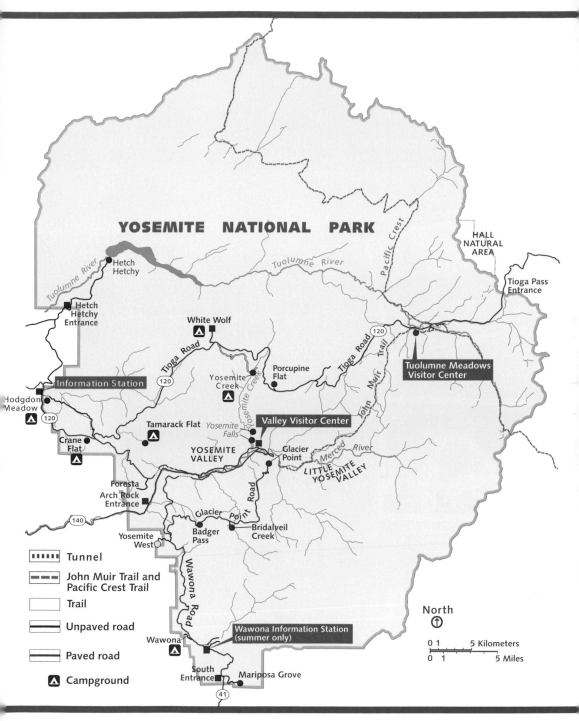

YOSEMITE NATIONAL PARK

HALL NATURAL AREA

Tuolumne River

Pacific Crest

Tioga Pass Entrance

Hetch Hetchy

Tuolumne River

Hetch Hetchy Entrance

White Wolf

Tioga Road

Porcupine Flat

Tuolumne Meadows Visitor Center

120

Information Station

Yosemite Creek

Tioga Road

120

John Muir Trail

Hodgdon Meadow

120

Tamarack Flat

Yosemite Creek

Yosemite Falls

Valley Visitor Center

Crane Flat

YOSEMITE VALLEY

Glacier Point

Merced River

LITTLE YOSEMITE VALLEY

Foresta

Arch Rock Entrance

140

Point Road

Glacier Point

Badger Pass

Bridalveil Creek

Yosemite West

Wawona Road

North

John Muir Trail and Pacific Crest Trail

Wawona Information Station (summer only)

Wawona

South Entrance

Mariposa Grove

41

▪▪▪▪▪▪	Tunnel
▬ ▬ ▬	John Muir Trail and Pacific Crest Trail
▭	Trail
▭	Unpaved road
▭	Paved road
▲	Campground

0 1   5 Kilometers
0 1   5 Miles

▲ *This map shows Yosemite National Park and some of its main points of interest.*

YOSEMITE NATIONAL

Location: Sierra Nevada, California

Date established: 1864: Yosemite Grant 1864 (state park)

Yosemite National Park: October 1, 1890 (areas surrounding state park)

Yosemite National Park and Yosemite Grant are combined: 1906

Area: 760,917 acres (307,932 hectares) / (1,189 square miles, 3,080 square kilometers), nearly the size of Rhode Island

Annual number of visitors: (2005) 3.4 million, 20,000 per day on the busiest summer days

Highest annual number: 4.2 million (1996)

Main areas of interest: Yosemite Valley, Glacier Point, Mariposa Grove, Hetch Hetchy Valley, Tuolumne Meadows, Tioga Pass, Wawona

Geologic features: Granite monoliths: Half Dome, El Capitan

Main waterfalls: Yosemite Falls, Vernal Fall, Bridalveil Fall, Nevada Fall, Sentinel Fall

Giant Sequoias: Mariposa Grove, Tuolumne Grove, Merced Grove

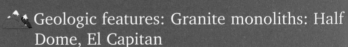

- Main rivers: Merced, Tuolumne

- Native trees: Chaparral in foothill woodland zone; mixed conifer forests and giant sequoia groves in lower montane forest; red fir, lodgepole pine, Jeffrey pine in uppermontane forest; western white pine and mountain hemlock in subalpine forest; above timberline in the alpine zone, trees cannot survive in the harsh climate and thin soil.

- Native animals and birds:

  Birds: raven, Steller's jay, mountain chickadee, Clark's nutcracker, gray-crowned rosy finch, American dipper, blue grouse, many kinds of owls, including the California spotted owl and the great gray owl, peregrine falcon, several kinds of woodpeckers, and many others

  Mammals: black bears, mountain lions, bighorn sheep, mule deer, bobcats, coyotes, gray foxes, chipmunks, squirrels, marmots, weasels, pikas, and many other small creatures

- Climate: Mediterranean climate: long, hot, dry summers, mild winters (long, cold winters at higher elevations with heavy snow)

- Scenic drives: Northside Drive and Southside Drive in Yosemite Valley, Glacier Point Road, Tioga Pass Road, Wawona Road

Chapter

1

The fog begins to clear in the valley below North Dome in Yosemite National Park. North Dome was a vantage point from which John Muir fell in love with the park.

Nature's Grandest Temple

John Muir, the world-renowned great conservationist and wilderness explorer, arrived in San Francisco in March 1868. He immediately asked for the nearest way out of town. Saying he wished to go "to any place that is wild,"[1] he was directed to the Oakland ferry. On April 1, Muir set out on foot for California's Sierra Nevada, the mountain range he would spend many years exploring. He specifically wanted to visit Yosemite, a place he had read about.

When Muir reached Yosemite and beheld the region's geologic and scenic wonders, he was stunned by the area's unique beauty. He later described Yosemite Valley as the "grandest of all the special temples of nature."[2]

Perched atop North Dome, several thousand feet above the floor of Yosemite Valley, Muir gazed in awe at the amazing spectacle before his eyes. He wrote:

> It is easier to feel than to realize, or in any way explain, Yosemite grandeur. The magnitudes of the rocks and trees and streams are so delicately harmonized they are mostly hidden. Sheer precipices three thousand feet high are fringed with tall trees growing close like grass on the brow of a lowland hill, and extending along the feet of these precipices a ribbon of meadow a mile wide and seven or eight long, that seems like a strip a farmer might mow in less than a day. Waterfalls, five hundred to one or two thousand feet high, are so subordinated to the mighty cliffs over which they pour that they seem like wisps of smoke, gentle as floating clouds, though their voices fill the valley and make the rocks tremble. The mountains, too, along the eastern sky, and the domes in front of them, and the succession of smooth rounded waves between, swelling higher, higher, with dark woods in their hollows, serene in massive exuberant bulk and beauty, tend yet more to hide the grandeur of the Yosemite temple and make it appear as a subdued subordinate feature of the vast harmonious landscape.[3]

⊜ AN ACCESSIBLE WILDERNESS

Yosemite is famous for its spectacular wild scenery. People come from all over the world to see the park's craggy peaks, sheer cliffs, massive granite domes, deep valleys, tall waterfalls, groves of giant sequoia trees, alpine meadows, and thousands of lakes and ponds. Also within the park are 1,600 miles (2,575 kilometers) of streams. The Merced and Tuolumne Rivers, both federally designated wild and scenic rivers, have their sources within the borders of Yosemite and flow west into California's Great Central Valley.

Yosemite National Park's 1,189 square miles (3,080 square kilometers) contain 196 miles (315 kilometers) of primary road and more than 800 miles (1,287 kilometers) of trails. Thus, Yosemite's scenic attractions are easily accessible to the park's more than 3 million annual visitors. Every effort has been made to accommodate even those visitors with special needs. Wheelchair rentals are available at the Yosemite Medical Clinic and at the Yosemite Lodge bike rental kiosk. Sign language interpreters are available during the summer months for visitors who are hearing impaired. And for those who are sight impaired, tactile exhibits can be found at the Yosemite Valley Visitor Center, Happy Isles Nature Center, Indian Cultural Museum, and Mariposa Grove Museum.

Many would argue that Yosemite, if anything, has actually become too accessible. After all, the park is less than a four-hour drive from the San Francisco Bay Area. And just about all of California's residents live within a one-day drive of

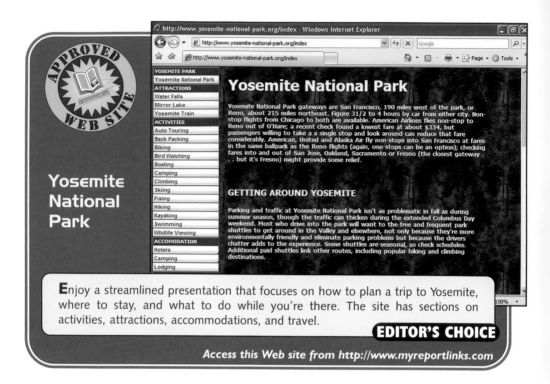

http://www.yosemite-national-park.org/index - Windows Internet Explorer

http://www.yosemite-national-park.org/index

http://www.yosemite-national-park.org/index

YOSEMITE PARK
Yosemite National Park

ATTRACTIONS
Water Falls
Mirror Lake
Yosemite Train

ACTIVITIES
Auto Touring
Back Packing
Biking
Bird Watching
Boating
Camping
Climbing
Skiing
Fising
Hiking
Kayaking
Swimming
Wildlife Viewing

ACCOMODATION
Hotels
Camping
Lodging

Yosemite National Park

Yosemite National Park gateways are San Francisco, 190 miles west of the park, or Reno, about 215 miles northeast. Figure 31/2 to 4 hours by car from either city. Non-stop flights from Chicago to both are available. American Airlines flies non-stop to Reno out of O'Hare; a recent check found a lowest fare at about $334, but passengers willing to take a a single stop and look around can reduce that fare considerably. American, United and Alaska Air fly non-stops into San Francisco at fares in the same ballpark as the Reno flights (again, one-stops can be an option); checking fares into and out of San Jose, Oakland, Sacramento or Fresno (the closest gateway . . . but it's Fresno) might provide some relief.

GETTING AROUND YOSEMITE

Parking and traffic at Yosemite National Park isn't as problematic in fall as during summer season, though the traffic can thicken during the extended Columbus Day weekend. Most who drive into the park will want to the free and frequent park shuttles to get around in the Valley and elsewhere, not only because they're more environmentally friendly and eliminate parking problems but because the drivers chatter adds to the experience. Some shuttles are seasonal, so check schedules. Additional paid shuttles link other routes, including popular hiking and climbing destinations.

Yosemite National Park

Enjoy a streamlined presentation that focuses on how to plan a trip to Yosemite, where to stay, and what to do while you're there. The site has sections on activities, attractions, accommodations, and travel.

EDITOR'S CHOICE

Access this Web site from http://www.myreportlinks.com

Yosemite. So the roads in Yosemite Valley, especially on busy summer days, experience heavy automobile traffic. The sweet mountain air can be tinged with the smell of exhaust fumes. On the busiest weekends, people throng the trails leading to the valley's various waterfalls. One wonders what John Muir would say had he been able to witness what has become of his wilderness paradise.

But while the traffic and the crowds can sometimes be annoying in the most popular areas during the busiest summer weekends, they really do little to diminish the wonder of Yosemite's beauty. And it is only right that all who wish to visit Yosemite can easily do so. And those who, like John Muir, seek to experience the solitude of the wilderness can still easily do so. Over 95 percent of Yosemite is designated wilderness, yet more than 95 percent of park visitors never walk more than 1/4 mile from the paved areas. Even in Yosemite Valley, and even on the busiest weekends, it is possible to be alone in the forest if you are willing to walk a relatively short distance. And, of course, in the vast reaches of Yosemite's high country, you can follow the John Muir Trail and other trails across the high mountain passes and gaze upon the same sparkling alpine lakes that so pleased the great explorer.

⇒ YOSEMITE VALLEY

Yosemite Valley is the part of the park that attracts the most visitors. The deep valley is about seven miles (11.2 kilometers) long and about one mile (1.6 kilometers) wide.

According to writer Tim Palmer:

> Yosemite National Park may be the scenic highlight of America, and Yosemite Valley is the highlight of the park. The Valley is the elegant climax to the entire Sierra, and, for that matter, to anything. Cliffs rise skyward. Waterfalls leap over the rim to be pushed aside by winds and then to smash onto rocks and hiss outward as riffling rivers, bubbling, glistening, perfectly clear. Ponderosa pines put on the weight of cambium easily and achieve a statuesque thickness in shady groves at meadow

The California Travel & Tourism Commission presents **Visit California**, a visitor's guide covering the state's regions, things to do, and how to get around. The site highlights the High Sierra region, which includes Yosemite Village.

EDITOR'S CHOICE

edges. And the meadows—they stretch up and down. From their centers the world of cliffs, waterfalls, and forests seems to revolve as in the kaleidoscope of childhood dreams, pure landscape fantasy, the kinds of dreams one might choose to die with given adequate presence of mind. Put simply, Yosemite Valley is for many people a vision of Eden, of heaven, of paradise.[4]

J. Smeaton Chase, an early explorer of the High Sierra, would have preferred that Yosemite Valley be called Yosemite Gorge because of its near-vertical walls. He wrote that:

The Yosemite Valley is not, properly speaking, a valley. That word conveys the image of a gentle depression with sloping sides, which the patient fingers of Time have smoothed and rounded into quiet, compliant lines. The Yosemite is not in the least of that character. It is a great cleft, or chasm, which one might imagine to have been the work of some exasperated Titan who, standing with feet planted fifty miles apart lengthwise of the Sierra Nevada summit and facing westward, raised his hands palm to palm over his head, and struck upon the earth with such fury as to cleave a gap nearly a mile in depth; then separating his hands he thrust back the sides of the fracture, leaving between them a narrow, precipice-walled plain.[5]

Among Yosemite Valley's amazing sights is 3,593-foot- (1,095-meter-) high El Capitan. Towering over the valley floor, El Capitan is the largest single chunk of granite in the world. Half Dome, even taller than El Capitan, rises nearly a mile above the valley floor. Yosemite's monumental granite domes make the valley a world-class destination for experienced rock climbers. Yosemite Falls, the tallest waterfall in North America and the fifth highest in the world, drops 2,425 feet (739 meters) into the valley. Bridalveil Fall tumbles 620 feet (189 meters).

The tops of Yosemite's huge granite domes provide some of the most incredible views of Yosemite Valley. But not every visitor is ready to climb up the sheer rock walls of the domes in

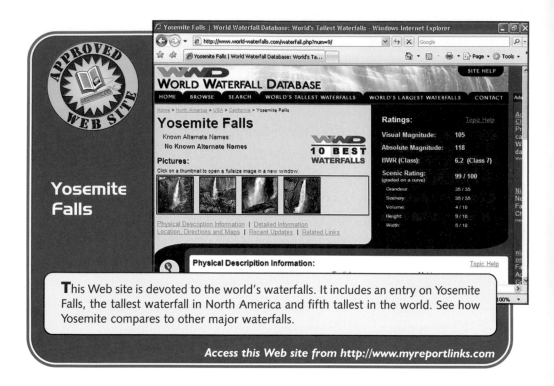

This Web site is devoted to the world's waterfalls. It includes an entry on Yosemite Falls, the tallest waterfall in North America and fifth tallest in the world. See how Yosemite compares to other major waterfalls.

Access this Web site from http://www.myreportlinks.com

order to view the valley from above. And many visitors to Yosemite are not able or willing to undertake strenuous hikes. Fortunately, people lacking the time or energy for hiking can drive their cars right up to Glacier Point, high above the valley. Visitors without a car can reach Yosemite's most famous viewpoint by tour bus.

The spectacular view from the Glacier Point overlook, at an elevation of 7,214 feet (2,199 meters), is often referred to as "the grandest view in all the West."[6] The sweeping view includes the valley floor about 3,200 feet (975 meters) below, the giant granite domes, including Half Dome, the various waterfalls, including Yosemite, Nevada, and Vernal Falls, and the distant peaks of the High Sierra. The Ahwahnee Hotel and Curry Village are clearly visible on the valley floor, which is laid out like a map at your feet. The Merced River can be seen snaking across the valley through meadows and forests.

→ GIANTS IN THE EARTH

The Mariposa Grove of giant sequoias is found at the southern boundary of Yosemite. It is the largest and most popular of Yosemite's three sequoia groves. The other two are the Tuolumne Grove and the Merced Grove. Writer Tim Palmer described his impressions of the Mariposa Grove upon arriving there at dusk. "The enormous girth and height of the trees were accentuated when the sequoias turned to black etchings against a navy blue, twilight sky. Lacking meaningful perspective in that forest full of mammoth trees, I walked up to one, spread my arms against its furrowed bark, and felt only the slightest turn of a curve in the trunk. It is difficult to hug a sequoia tree—the largest organism on earth."[7]

Some of the giant sequoia trees are almost 300 feet (91 meters) tall. They are also among the oldest living things. Grizzly Giant is the largest of the approximately five hundred sequoias in the Mariposa Grove. While "only" 210 feet (64 meters) tall, it is 31 feet (9.5 meters) thick at its base. While there is some discussion regarding the diameter of the Grizzly Giant, it is most often considered to be between 27 and 29 feet (8.2 to 8.8 meters) in diameter. Its huge branches are bigger in circumference than most of the pines in the forest. Grizzly Giant is also very old, having lived for an estimated 1,800 years.

Horace Greeley, editor and publisher of the *New York Tribune*, visited the Mariposa Grove in 1859. "Here," he wrote, "the Big Trees have been quietly nestled for I dare not say how many thousand years." But "that they were of very substantial size when David danced before the ark, when Solomon laid the foundations of the Temple, when Theseus ruled in Athens, when Aeneas fled from the burning wreck of vanquished Troy, when Sesostris led his victorious Egyptians into the heart of Asia," he had "no manner of doubt."[8]

In 1871, John Muir took the famous American essayist and poet Ralph Waldo Emerson to see the Mariposa Grove. Muir wrote, "We . . . stayed an hour or two, mostly in ordinary tourist fashion—looking at the biggest giants, measuring them with a tape line, riding through prostrate fire-bored trunks, etc., though Mr. Emerson was alone occasionally, sauntering about as if under a spell. As we walked through a fine group, he quoted, 'There were giants in those days,' recognizing the antiquity of the race."[9]

▲ *Mariposa Grove (shown here) is the most popular sequoia grove in Yosemite National Park.*

➡ BEAR COUNTRY

A drawing of a grizzly bear by the artist Charles Nahl appears on the state flag of California. At one time, there were large numbers of brown bears, known as grizzlies, in the Yosemite region and other parts of California. But the grizzly population in California fell rapidly as human settlement expanded. Because the ferocious grizzly bear is regarded as an important part of California's heritage, the state legislature in 1953 named the grizzly bear the official state animal. But by that time, the grizzly had already become extinct in the state. The last grizzly in Yosemite was killed in 1895 at Wawona in the southwestern part of the park. The last grizzly in the state was shot to death in 1922 in Fresno County.

Black bears, however, are still quite numerous in Yosemite. Many visitors to Yosemite have sighted them. Compared to grizzlies, black bears are peaceful creatures. But while nobody has ever been killed by a black bear in Yosemite, some people have been injured. To avoid problems when encountering bears, hikers and campers are advised to take certain precautions. If you should meet a black bear along a trail, do not drop your backpack. And do not run, which will most likely cause the bear to chase you. And the bear will outrun you. Unprovoked black bear attacks on humans are extremely rare. But if it

Although they are extinct there now, grizzlies played a big role in Yosemite's history. Here, Defenders of Wildlife offers a description of the grizzly, its status in the wild, and the threats it faces.

Access this Web site from http://www.myreportlinks.com

should happen, you must fight back any way you can. Throw stones or sticks, or hit the bear with your gear.

When in Yosemite, you need to be especially careful about how you store your food. Over the years, the black bears in Yosemite have gotten used to humans and have lost some of their natural fear of us. They have a keen sense of smell and are attracted by food odors. They can even smell food that is sealed in plastic or foil. They also can look in windows and recognize food packaging. For many years, the bears have made a habit of raiding refuse disposal areas in the park. They have also been known to invade tents while the human occupants

There are many black bears throughout the park. Rangers ask visitors to be careful with their food so that they do not provoke encounters with the bears.

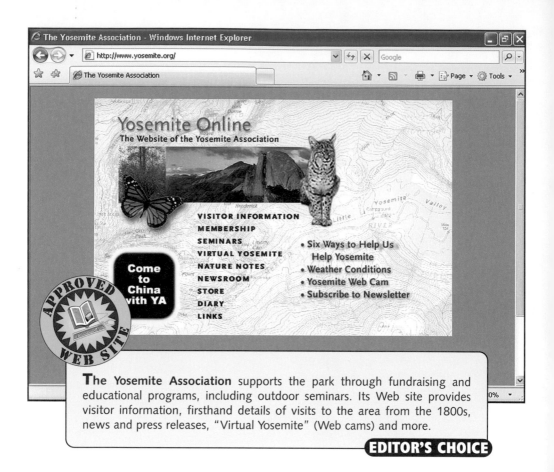

The Yosemite Association - Windows Internet Explorer

http://www.yosemite.org/

Google

The Yosemite Association

Page ▾ Tools ▾

Yosemite Online
The Website of the Yosemite Association

VISITOR INFORMATION
MEMBERSHIP
SEMINARS
VIRTUAL YOSEMITE
NATURE NOTES
NEWSROOM
STORE
DIARY
LINKS

Come to China with YA

- Six Ways to Help Us Help Yosemite
- Weather Conditions
- Yosemite Web Cam
- Subscribe to Newsletter

The Yosemite Association supports the park through fundraising and educational programs, including outdoor seminars. Its Web site provides visitor information, firsthand details of visits to the area from the 1800s, news and press releases, "Virtual Yosemite" (Web cams) and more.

EDITOR'S CHOICE

sleep. Hungry bears have often broken into locked cars to get at the food, smashing the windows and ripping up the seats. Campers are advised to store all food and even items such as gum, toothpaste, soap, lip gloss, and sunscreen in large metal storage lockers known as bear boxes. The bear-proof boxes are available at every Yosemite campsite at most parking areas in the park. The Park Service requires wilderness campers to use bear canisters, which are available for rent at visitor contact stations throughout the park. Failure to properly store food can result in a fine.

Many thousands of visitors camp in Yosemite each year. Because the campgrounds are usually full, it is sometimes easy to forget that Yosemite is a wild area. But campers must keep in mind that they are in the middle of the wilderness. Bears can appear at any time, seeming to come out of nowhere. When encountering a bear at a campsite, it is important that you do not panic. Clap your hands, wave your arms, yell, and bang pots together. The noise will most likely cause the bear to wander back into the woods. Most visitors to Yosemite are grateful for the chance to see bears in their native habitat. For many, an encounter with such a large, wild animal is a thrilling experience. Fortunately, Yosemite will continue to provide a taste of the wilderness for all who seek it.

Chapter

2

Geologists believe the Yosemite Valley was carved by moving glaciers that melted over millions of years.

History of the Yosemite Region

Visitors awestruck by Yosemite's stupendous rock formations and other geologic features may well wonder how such a fantastic region ever came to be. The forces of nature required to carve out Yosemite Valley, for example, must have been so tremendous as to defy the imagination. John Muir was the first to attempt a scientific explanation for the creation of the Yosemite region.

→ GEOLOGIC HISTORY: GIFT OF THE GLACIERS

John Muir had university training in geology. He studied under Ezra Carr, who had previously studied under the famous geologist Louis Agassiz. When Muir began exploring the Yosemite region, he followed the paths of the glaciers he discovered in the high country. He carefully measured the slow movement of the glaciers and thought about the effects of ice on the underlying rock. Muir found deposits of glacial silt and striations etched into granite formations. This evidence suggested to him that the valley had been shaped and scoured by successive waves of glaciation.

Muir became convinced that glaciers were indeed responsible for the major geological features of the Yosemite region. He wrote:

> No other mountain chain on the globe, as far as I know, is so rich as the Sierra in bold, striking, well-preserved glacial monuments, easily understood by anybody capable of patient observation. Every feature is more or less glacial, and this park portion of the range is the brightest and clearest of all. Not a peak, ridge, dome, cañon, lake basin, garden, forest, or stream but in some way explains the past existence and modes of action of flowing, grinding, sculpturing, soil-making, scenery-making ice.[1]

Muir studied lines and grooves in the polished rock surfaces in Yosemite's high country, best seen at elevations of 8,000 to 9,000 feet (2,438 to 2,743 meters). Muir referred to these rock surfaces as "pavements." He wrote that, "In the production of this admirable hard finish, the glaciers in many places exerted a pressure of more than a hundred tons to the square foot, planing down granite, slate, and quartz alike, showing

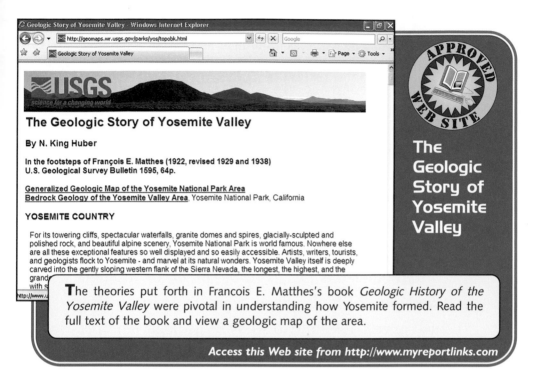

Access this Web site from http://www.myreportlinks.com

their structure, and making beautiful mosaics where large feldspar crystals form the greater part of the rock. On such pavements the sunshine is at times dazzling, as if the surface were of burnished silver."[2]

California State Geologist Josiah D. Whitney thought Muir's theory of glaciation to be utter nonsense. Whitney argued that Yosemite Valley was formed by a single, great cataclysmic event during which the bottom of the valley dropped. According to Whitney, Half Dome was created at the same time when a much larger dome was sheared in half. In his *Yosemite Guide-book* published in 1869, Whitney wrote:

A more absurd theory was never advanced than
that by which it was sought to ascribe to glaciers
the sawing out of those vertical walls and the
rounding of the domes. . . . There is no reason to
suppose, or at least no proof, that glaciers have
ever occupied the Valley, or any portion of it . . . so
that this theory, based on entire ignorance of the
whole subject, may be dropped without wasting
any more time of it.[3]

Since Muir's time, many scientists who studied
the area proposed their own theories. At least a
dozen other theories as to the origin of Yosemite
were put forth. Over the years, scientists continued to visit Yosemite to study its geologic features.
Finally in 1930, Francois E. Matthes, a geologist
with the U.S. Geological Survey, settled the mat-
ter. In his *Geologic History of the Yosemite Valley*,
Matthes combined elements of these various
theories in a comprehensive new theory. Matthes
basically agreed with Muir's theory of glaciation.
He proposed that most of the depth of the valley
was originally gouged by water erosion. But glacial action then widened and shaped the valley.
Matthes's theory became the accepted version of
how Yosemite was created.

According to the current theory, the geological
processes that created Yosemite began their work
about 400 million years ago. Scientists believe
that at that time, the land that is now the Sierra
Nevada, including the Yosemite region, lay

beneath an ancient sea. Layers of sedimentary rock, thousands of feet thick, were eventually thrust upward by movements of the Pacific and North American continental plates. The rock layers pushed up above the surface of the sea, forming a new mountain range.

Then, during a period of volcanic activity, molten rock rose from deep within the earth below the mountain range. The molten rock cooled beneath the overlying layer of sedimentary rock, forming an immense block of granite. Geologists refer to this granite as the Sierra Nevada Batholith. Over millions of years, weathering and erosion

▲ *Half Dome is one of the most popular peaks in Yosemite. Scientists have argued over how Half Dome was formed.*

wore away most of the surface sedimentary rock, exposing the granite underneath. Today, most of the rock in Yosemite is granite, including the massive domes.

About 10 million years ago, another major uplift of the Sierra Nevada occurred. The entire block of the Sierra range was tilted to the west. This resulted in a long, gentle slope on the western side of the Sierra and a steep slope on the eastern side. Westward-flowing streams carved V-shaped valleys into the western slope.

Between 2 million and 3 million years ago, the earth entered an ice age. Yosemite and much of the rest of the Sierra range were buried under thick glaciers. Ice filled the V-shaped valleys, and when the ice moved, it sculpted them into U-shaped canyons. The ice may have been up to 4,000 feet (1,219 meters) deep. The downslope movement of the massive rivers of ice carved out Yosemite Valley and shaped other canyons in the area. One of these is Hetch Hetchy Valley, just to the north of Yosemite Valley. The name "Hetch Hetchy" comes from the Miwok Indian name "Hatchatchie," a type of grass with edible seeds that grew there. Hetch Hetchy was remarkably similar to Yosemite Valley, and was said to be just as beautiful. Hetch Hetchy could almost be viewed as Yosemite Valley's twin, except that it is now partially filled with water. O'Shaughnessy Dam was

Camping in the park is a favorite activity among park visitors. This tent was pitched in the Hetch Hetchy Valley.

built on the Tuolumne River in Hetch Hetchy Valley during the years 1914 to 1923. The dam and reservoir provide some of the water and hydroelectric power for the city of San Francisco and other parts of the Bay Area.

The glaciers rounded out the contours of many of Yosemite's landscape features, such as the granite domes that lay beneath the ice. The mighty force of the glaciers removed weaker or softer rock, grinding it into rubble. Geologists believe there were at least four major glaciations; periods of advancing and retreating glaciers. The last glaciation ended about ten thousand years ago.

Exfoliation, the tendency of granite to crack and separate, is an ongoing geologic process in Yosemite. The massive granite rock formations expand and crack in shell-like layers. This happens when the pressure on the granite from overlying sediment is removed as the sediment erodes away. The surfaces of the granite formations then become smoother and even more rounded. The process of exfoliation is still at work.

Gravity, another force of nature, produces still more geologic changes in Yosemite. Every so often, sections of the rock walls of Yosemite Valley break away, resulting in rock slides and rockfalls. Some rock slides have been massive. On July 10, 1996, an eighty-thousand-ton slab of granite broke off the southeast side of Glacier Point. The rock plunged over one thousand feet (305 meters) down the sheer vertical rock wall and crashed onto the valley floor.

The various forces of nature affecting Yosemite's landscape continue their work. There are even a few small glaciers, including Lyell Glacier, still existing in the park. Covering an area of 160 acres (65 hectares), Lyell Glacier is the largest glacier in the Sierra Nevada. Due to global warming, many of Yosemite's former glaciers, including Merced Glacier, discovered by John Muir in 1871, no longer exist. Other glaciers in Yosemite have lost up to 75 percent of their surface area. Little by little, Yosemite's appearance changes as the years go by.

➔ YOSEMITE'S FIRST HUMAN INHABITANTS

During the last Ice Age, sea levels were much lower. During this period of glaciation, a land bridge extended across the Bering Strait, connecting Alaska and Siberia. Scientists believe that between twenty thousand and forty thousand years ago, nomadic hunters began migrating from Asia to North America. They followed herds of wild animals across the land bridge. By about 10,000 B.C., the Ice Age was ending. The thick sheets of ice covering much of North America were retreating. Groups of nomadic hunters, called Paleo-Indians by archeologists, wandered south. They hunted

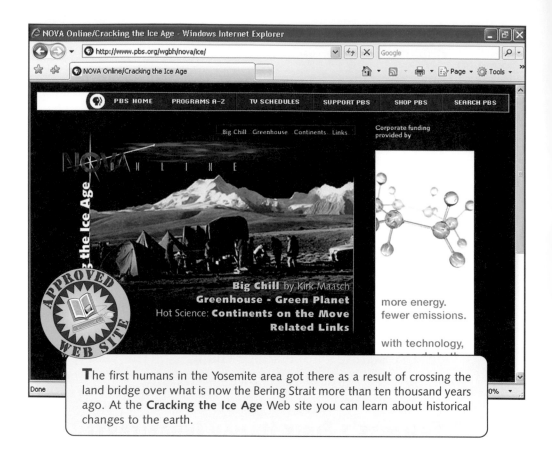

The first humans in the Yosemite area got there as a result of crossing the land bridge over what is now the Bering Strait more than ten thousand years ago. At the **Cracking the Ice Age** Web site you can learn about historical changes to the earth.

animals such as the now-extinct woolly mammoth, mastodon, and giant ground sloth.

Archaeologists believe the first Paleo-Indians entered what is now California around 10,000 B.C. Archaeologists have discovered ancient arrowheads in California thought to be about twelve thousand years old. Paleo-Indians may have first visited Yosemite as early as ten thousand years ago. Around 2000 B.C., a Southern Sierra Miwok tribe became the first people to settle in Yosemite Valley. They called the valley

Ahwahnee, a wonderfully descriptive name that means "valley that looks like a gaping mouth." They called themselves the Ahwahneechee, which means "dwellers in Ahwahnee."

The Ahwahneechee were hunter-gatherers. They lived in harmony with nature. The grizzly bear was an important element of their mythology. Food was plentiful in Yosemite Valley. The Ahwahneechee hunted bear, deer, and squirrels with bows and arrows. They snared birds, and netted and speared trout in the Merced River. They gathered nuts and berries. The Ahwahneechee's single most important food was acorns gathered from the black oaks in the valley. The Ahwahneechee ground the acorns into flour for hotcakes, gruel, and mush. First they poured boiling water over the acorn flour to leach out the tannic acid. Each year in the fall, the Ahwahneechee set fire to the grasses in the valley. This prevented the dense forest from spreading over the meadows and competing with the black oaks. Keeping the meadows open also made hunting and gathering easier.

For many centuries, the Ahwahneechee enjoyed a relatively peaceful life in their beautiful valley. They followed their age-old traditional ways. They made baskets from willow, ferns, and strips of bark. They made tools such as knives and scrapers from bones and antlers. The Ahwahneechee traded with the Mono Paiute people on the eastern side of

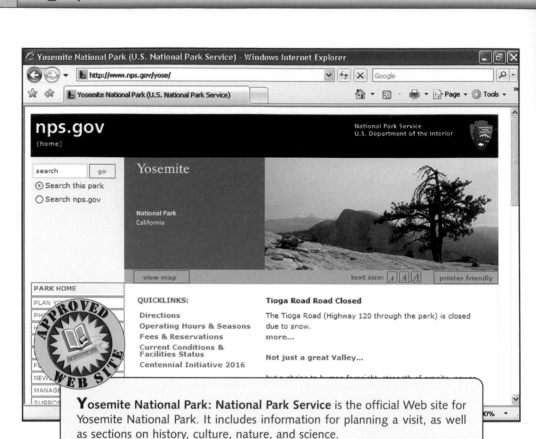

nps.gov
(home)

National Park Service
U.S. Department of the Interior

search [go]

⊙ Search this park
○ Search nps.gov

Yosemite

National Park
California

[view map]

text size: A A A   [printer friendly]

PARK HOME
PLAN YO...
PH...

QUICKLINKS:

Directions
Operating Hours & Seasons
Fees & Reservations
Current Conditions &
Facilities Status
Centennial Initiative 2016

NEW...
MANAGE...
SUPPOR...

Tioga Road Road Closed

The Tioga Road (Highway 120 through the park) is closed
due to snow.
more...

Not just a great Valley...

Yosemite National Park: National Park Service is the official Web site for
Yosemite National Park. It includes information for planning a visit, as well
as sections on history, culture, nature, and science.

EDITOR'S CHOICE

the Sierra. In exchange for acorns and seashells,
the Ahwahneechee got salt, obsidian, and pine
nuts. But eventually something happened that
would forever change life for the Ahwahneechee
and other native California people—the coming of
the white man.

➡ THE ARRIVAL OF EUROPEANS

In 1769, Father Junípero Serra and a few other
Franciscan padres traveled north from New Spain,
which is now Mexico. They established a mission
in what is now San Diego. They eventually built

twenty-one missions up and down the coast of California. The Spaniards invited the local American Indian peoples into the missions and converted them to Christianity while forcing them to work for them.

Unfortunately, the Spaniards also passed along European diseases to which the natives had no immunity. These diseases included diphtheria, smallpox, pneumonia, syphilis, and others. Around 1800, an epidemic of either cholera or smallpox spread among native peoples as far as Yosemite Valley. Few Ahwahneechees survived the plague. Those who did fled the valley, leaving their villages uninhabited to join nearby tribes.

In the autumn of 1833, Joseph Reddeford Walker led a group of seventy hunters and trappers across the High Sierra. They were traveling from east to west, having begun their expedition near the Green River in Utah. Their route passed along the north rim of Yosemite Valley. Zenas Leonard, Walker's clerk, described this part of their journey: "We travelled a few miles every day, still on top of the mountain, and our course continually obstructed by snow, hills and rocks. Here we began to encounter in our path many small streams which would shoot out from under these high snowbanks, and after running a short distance in deep chasms they have through ages cut through the rock, precipitate themselves from one lofty precipice to another, until they were exhausted in rain below. Some of these precipices appeared to us to be more than a mile high."[4]

Unable to descend the cliffs of the northern wall of Yosemite Valley, Walker and his men camped on its rim. They are believed to be the first white men to see Yosemite, although they never entered the valley.

A few days later, the Walker group was traveling at a lower elevation when they happened upon what is thought to have been either the Tuolumne or Merced Grove of giant sequoia trees. They became the first known nonindigenous people to see the giant trees. Leonard wrote that they saw "trees of the Redwood species, incredibly large, some of which would measure from 16 to 18 fathoms around the trunk at the height of a man's head above the ground."[5]

In January 1848, gold was discovered at Sutter's Mill, near present-day Sacramento. Before long, thousands of prospectors descended on the gold fields of California, hoping to get rich. The newcomers swept through the foothills of the Sierra Nevada. The miners had no respect for the rights of the native peoples of the area. They trespassed on native hunting grounds, killed animals, chopped down trees, and filled salmon streams with silt. The main food sources of American Indians were soon destroyed.

Father Junípero Serra was a Spanish missionary who set up missions throughout the region once known as New Spain. The area that is now Yosemite National Park was once part of New Spain. This statue of Father Serra is located in California, although not in Yosemite.

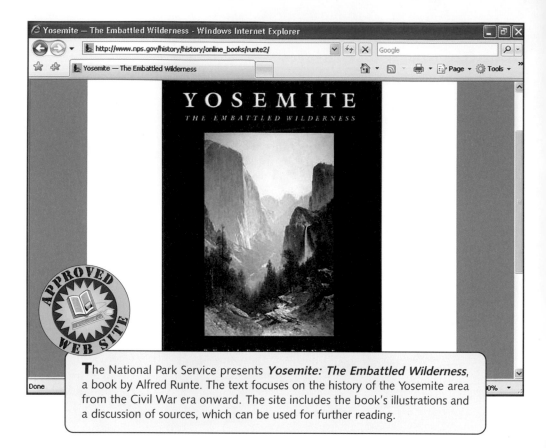

The National Park Service presents *Yosemite: The Embattled Wilderness*, a book by Alfred Runte. The text focuses on the history of the Yosemite area from the Civil War era onward. The site includes the book's illustrations and a discussion of sources, which can be used for further reading.

On October 18, 1849, William P. Abrams and a companion wandered as far as Yosemite Valley. Abrams provided accurate descriptions of some of the valley's landmarks. But it is not known if he actually entered the valley. The following year, Joseph Screech became the first white man to enter Hetch Hetchy Valley. He fell in love with the place and settled there.

➔ THE SAD STORY OF CHIEF TENAYA

Abrams and Screech may or may not have been aware of the fact that Ahwahneechee Indians were once again living in Yosemite Valley. Sometime before 1851, Chief Tenaya and about two hundred Ahwahneechee had resettled the valley. Tenaya had grown up among the Paiute people in the Mono Lake region, east of the Sierra. Tenaya's father, an Ahwahneechee chief, had told him about the magnificent former home of their people. Tenaya visited Yosemite Valley and, finding it free of disease, led the Ahwahneechees back to Yosemite.

It did not take long for misfortune to befall Chief Tenaya and his people. During the gold rush, it became clear that the interests of gold seekers and native peoples clashed. Skirmishes around the outskirts of Yosemite Valley became common. In 1851, California governor John McDougall called for a war of extermination against the American Indians. At the very least, miners and settlers demanded that California's ten thousand native peoples be confined to reservations.

In January 1851, a miner named James D. Savage accused the Yosemite Indians of attacking his trading post along the Merced River. Savage formed a small army of militiamen, calling it the Mariposa Battalion. Savage then set out to round up the Ahwahneechees in Yosemite Valley. Just outside the valley, Savage met up with Tenaya and a group of Indians. He warned the chief that unless he and his people agreed to relocate to a reservation near Fresno they would all be killed.

Tenaya Lake is one of many landmarks in Yosemite named after Ahwahneechee chief Tenaya.

On March 27, 1851, Savage and his army proceeded into Yosemite Valley. There they set up camp on the valley floor. Lafayette Bunnell, a member of the Mariposa Battalion, kept a diary of the expedition. He was overcome with emotion upon first glimpsing the scenic splendor of Yosemite Valley. Bunnell wrote, "The grandeur of the scene was but softened by the haze that hung over the valley—light as gossamer—and by the clouds which partially dimmed the higher cliffs and mountains. This obscurity of vision but increased the awe with which I beheld it, and as I looked, a peculiar exalted sensation seemed to fill my whole being, and I found my eyes in tears with emotion."[6]

Meanwhile, the Ahwahneechee had fled their village before the arrival of Savage and his army. Tenaya had also escaped. Savage was unable to round up the Indians, who had gone into hiding. Savage burned the Ahwahneechee village but ultimately failed to carry out his mission. Soon after, in May 1851, a second expedition under the command of John Boling succeeded in hunting down and capturing Chief Tenaya and the Ahwahneechees. The youngest of Tenaya's three sons was killed while trying to escape.

The Ahwahneechee were very unhappy on the reservation near Fresno. They suffered from the hot weather and the poor food they were given,

▲ *Today, the Merced River is a place of quiet tranquility. Though, at one time trader James Savage accused Yosemite Indians of attacking his trading post along the Merced. This led to tension between the American Indians and white settlers of the area.*

but most of all from their lack of freedom. When Chief Tenaya asked for permission to return to Yosemite, the Indian agent granted his request. But Tenaya first had to promise not to cause any more trouble.

Tenaya and the Ahwahneechee returned to Yosemite Valley. But they would not stay there for long. In the spring of 1852, several Ahwahneechees attacked a group of prospectors in the valley, killing two of them. The U.S. Army sent a detachment of soldiers into Yosemite Valley. The soldiers captured five American Indians supposedly guilty of killing the miners and executed them. Tenaya and some followers fled over the High Sierra to Mono Lake. There they stayed with the Mono Paiutes. The following year, in the summer of 1853, Chief Tenaya and several other Ahwahneechees were killed by the Paiutes in a fight that broke out during a gambling game.

Sadly, the Ahwahneechee had met their demise. The remaining members of Tenaya's tribe scattered. Some joined the Paiute, some joined Miwok tribes along the Tuolumne River. A few Ahwahneechees continued to live in Yosemite Valley. Chief Tenaya's name lives on in Yosemite at Tenaya Lake, Tenaya Creek, Tenaya Canyon, and Tenaya Lodge.

A VALLEY NAMED YOSEMITE

Lafayette Bunnell of the Mariposa Battalion had heard Chief Tenaya speak the Miwok word *uzumate*. Believing this was the Ahwahneechee word for "grizzly bear" and also the name for their valley, Bunnell named it Yosemite Valley. For more

The Tuolomne River runs through Yosemite National Park. At one time, Miwok Indians lived along its banks.

than a hundred years, historians believed that Yosemite meant "grizzly bear." But eventually, they learned that Yosemite had a different meaning. It turns out that the Miwok word for grizzly is *husso*. According to Alfred Runte, "*Yosemite* is now believed to be a corruption of *Yo-che-ma-te*, literally meaning 'some among them are killers.' In any reference to the militia companies of March and May 1851, the meaning would be dramatically obvious. What the soldiers may have mistaken as a comparison of themselves to the revered grizzly bear may in fact have been a warning among members of Tenaya's band to fear for their very lives."[7]

⇒ TOURISTS DISCOVER YOSEMITE

In 1855 most Americans had not yet heard of Yosemite and its amazing scenery. But this was about to change. That year, an Englishman by the name of James Mason Hutchings visited Yosemite. Hutchings, a miner, had failed to become rich in the gold rush. But he still dreamed of finding fame and fortune in California. When he gazed at the wonders of Yosemite Valley, he had visions of the valley as a tourist mecca. He immediately published an account of his visit in the August 9, 1855 issue of the *Mariposa Gazette*.

Hutchings brought the artist Thomas A. Ayres with him to Yosemite. Ayres mapped out several illustrations of Yosemite Valley, including a drawing of Yosemite Falls. In the following year, Ayres visited Tuolumne Meadows in the high country of Yosemite. He made more drawings and wrote about his visit. That year, in July 1856, Hutchings published the first edition of his magazine *Hutchings' Illustrated California Magazine*. In it he included some of Ayres' drawings of Yosemite Valley. An art exhibition of Ayres' drawings was later held in New York City.

In 1859, Hutchings brought photographer Charles Leander Weed to Yosemite. Weed took the first photographs of Yosemite Valley. His photographs were exhibited in September of that year in San Francisco. During the next few years, Hutchings continued to publish articles and pictures of Yosemite in his magazine. The nation suddenly became aware of Yosemite. More and more people decided to see the amazing region for themselves. In more recent times, the striking images of Yosemite by the famous photographer Ansel Adams created fresh impressions of the region for millions of people.

Visitors began coming to Yosemite Valley and other parts of the area in the 1850s. An initial trickle of tourists grew into a steady stream of visitors. The tourists hoped to get a taste of wilderness and experience the beauties of nature. In 1859 Horace Greeley, the editor and publisher of the *New York Tribune*, visited Yosemite. The

This is the view you would see if you entered Yosemite National Park from the south driving along Route 41.

following year the Reverend Thomas Starr King of Boston took a horseback trip to Yosemite Valley. In 1863 the great American landscape painter Albert Bierstadt visited Yosemite Valley. There he sketched the valley's cliffs, domes, and waterfalls. The paintings of Bierstadt and other artists such as Thomas Hill and William Keith helped promote the vision of Yosemite as a special paradise awaiting visitors to the Sierra.

Meanwhile, a homesteader named Galen Clark had settled in the area that would later be called Wawona, in what is now the southwestern part of Yosemite National Park. In 1857, Clark and Milton Mann discovered the Mariposa Grove of giant sequoia trees near Wawona. The name "Wawona" is the Nutchu Indian word for the sound of the great horned owl, thought to be the spirit guardian of the big trees.

That same year, Milton and Houston Mann built a toll path up the South Fork of the Merced River and over to the floor of Yosemite Valley. Clark was sure that an increasing number of visitors would eventually make their way into Yosemite. So in 1857, Clark set up a stagecoach station and enlarged his small cabin to accommodate travelers, calling it Clark's Station. He also built a bridge over the South Fork of the Merced River in Wawona. As tourists began to arrive,

Clark acted as their guide to the "Big Trees" and the valley.

Other entrepreneurs began building roads and trails in Yosemite. In 1857 the first primitive lodging opened for guests in Yosemite Valley opposite Yosemite Falls. Two years later, the Upper Hotel, a more substantial structure, opened farther up the valley.

In 1859, James C. Lamon settled in the upper end of Yosemite Valley. He built a cabin, planted an orchard, and tended a garden. He planned to sell fruit and other produce to summer visitors. In 1863, James Hutchings bought the Upper Hotel.

➔ THE YOSEMITE GRANT

Some of the early visitors to Yosemite recognized that the area's unique beauty should belong to all Americans. They felt strongly that Yosemite Valley and its surroundings had to be protected. They believed that Yosemite should not be allowed to become the private property of developers and others intent on commercializing the area.

"The principal advocate of the idea [of a public park] was Captain Israel Ward Raymond, the California representative of the Central American Steamship Transit Company of New York. . . . On February 20, 1864, Raymond addressed a decisive letter to the junior senator from California, John Conness, urging Congress . . ."[8]

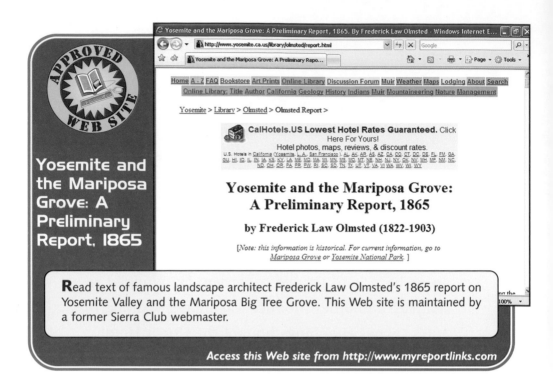

Yosemite and the Mariposa Grove: A Preliminary Report, 1865

Read text of famous landscape architect Frederick Law Olmsted's 1865 report on Yosemite Valley and the Mariposa Big Tree Grove. This Web site is maintained by a former Sierra Club webmaster.

Access this Web site from http://www.myreportlinks.com

Among those seeking to protect Yosemite was the Reverend Thomas Starr King. He was worried that the homesteading and commercial activity he observed in Yosemite would ruin the area. King expressed his concerns in his six travel letters published in the *Boston Evening Transcript* in 1860 and 1861. King became the first to call for the establishment of a public Yosemite park. Frederick Law Olmsted was instrumental in helping draft how the grant would be protected and managed. The bill passed both houses of Congress.

In 1864 the Civil War was still raging. President Abraham Lincoln's attention was focused on making sure the North won the war. But on June

30 of that year, Lincoln took the time to sign the Yosemite Grant Act into law. It created the Yosemite Grant as a public trust. Yosemite Valley and the Mariposa Grove of giant sequoias were deeded to California as a state park. Yosemite thus became the first state park in the world. Next would come the struggle for the creation of Yosemite National Park.

Chapter

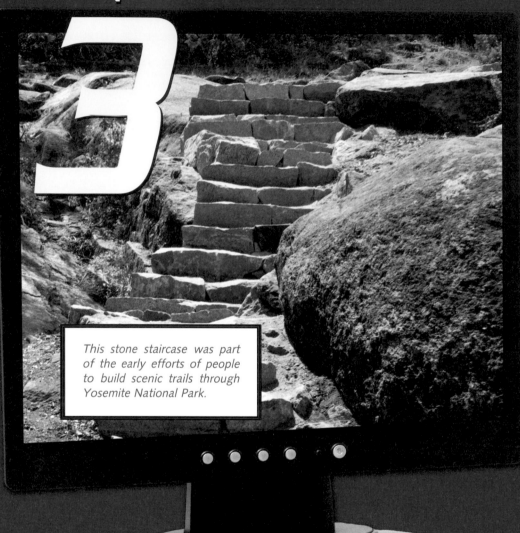

3

This stone staircase was part of the early efforts of people to build scenic trails through Yosemite National Park.

History of Yosemite National Park

Passage of the Yosemite Grant Act marked the first time a government mandated the preservation and protection of a wild natural area as a park for public use and recreation. But after Yosemite Valley and the Mariposa Grove became a state park, there were numerous challenges to its status.

As an increasing number of tourists visited the park, settlers such as James Lamon and James Hutchings sought to maintain private ownership of their property in the park. After several years of legal battles in Congress, Lamon and Hutchings had their land claims finally rejected by the United States Supreme Court in December 1872. Homesteading would no longer be permitted in the park.

Yet there were other problems. Many people were exploiting the land surrounding Yosemite Valley and the Mariposa Grove in various ways. Loggers were chopping down the giant sequoias and other big conifers. Hundreds of sawmills were built on the west slope of the Sierra. Miners seeking gold and silver set up operations in even the most remote areas. And in the summer, ranchers grazed their cattle and sheep in the fragile meadows of the high country.

As the number of visitors to Yosemite kept increasing, the number of concessions established to serve them continued to grow. These included a bakery, a store, and Camp Curry, now known as Curry Village, in Yosemite Valley. Galen Clark, who had been appointed as the park's first guardian, worked hard to make Yosemite more accessible. During the mid-1870s, three stagecoach roads to the park were built. More hotels were built.

YOSEMITE BECOMES A NATIONAL PARK

Among the visitors to Yosemite was John Muir, who arrived in 1868. Muir was so taken with the natural beauty of the area that he stayed. As the years went by, Muir thoroughly explored Yosemite Valley and the surrounding high country. Eventually, Muir and others concerned with the protection and preservation of the park, became alarmed at the pace of development. Muir saw

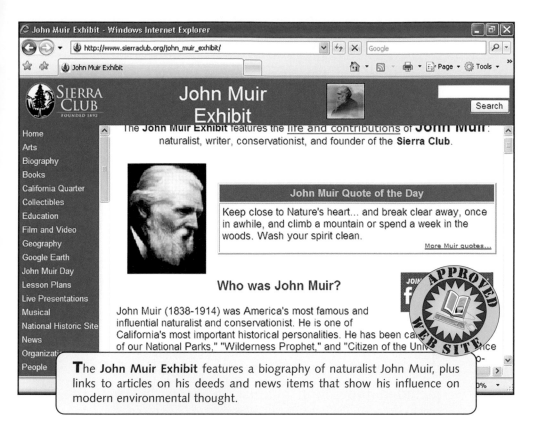

The **John Muir Exhibit** features a biography of naturalist John Muir, plus links to articles on his deeds and news items that show his influence on modern environmental thought.

that the various logging, mining, and grazing activities in the high country directly threatened the land within the park boundaries.

In 1889, Muir met Robert Underwood Johnson, the editor of *Century Magazine*. Muir took Johnson on a camping trip to Tuolumne Meadows in the high country above Yosemite Valley. He showed Johnson the damage from logging and overgrazing by sheep. Johnson agreed with Muir that something had to be done to protect the land. He told Muir, "Obviously, the thing to do was to make a Yosemite National Park around the Valley on the plan of the Yellowstone [National Park, created in 1872]."[1]

Muir wrote articles promoting the idea of establishing Yosemite National Park. Johnson published the articles in his magazine the following summer. Johnson argued persuasively for the creation of the park with influential members of Congress in Washington. On October 1, 1890, Congress passed the Yosemite Act of 1890, creating Yosemite National Park. This act withdrew lands from "settlement, occupancy, or sale" and protected "all timber, mineral deposits [none in Yosemite], natural curiosities or wonders, and their retention in their natural condition." This included protection against "wanton destruction of the fish and game, and their capture or destruction for purposes of merchandise or profit."[2]

The new Yosemite National Park was the third national park to be established in the United States. It included the watersheds of the Tuolumne and Merced Rivers and the land surrounding Yosemite Valley. But it did not include Yosemite Valley and the Mariposa Grove, which remained under state control. The new park was put under the jurisdiction of the Fourth Cavalry of the U.S. Army. The Army would remain in Yosemite until 1916. But the federal troops were not yet allowed into Yosemite Valley.

A huge proponent of the national park system, President Theodore Roosevelt visited Yosemite in 1903. ▷

Muir and Johnson realized that further protection would be needed. So in 1892, Muir founded the Sierra Club. The environmental organization's first major goal was to work for the inclusion of Yosemite Valley and the Mariposa Grove within Yosemite National Park. As president of the Sierra Club, Muir continued to lead the struggle to preserve Yosemite as a wilderness. In 1898, Muir wrote, "Thousands of nerve-shaken, overcivilized people are beginning to find out that going to the mountains is going home; that wilderness is a necessity; and that mountain parks and reservations are useful not only as fountains of timber and irrigating rivers, but as fountains of life."[3]

In May 1903, President Theodore Roosevelt visited Yosemite. Roosevelt had long been a lover of nature and admirer of the wilderness. Muir took Roosevelt on an overnight hike to Glacier Point. Roosevelt was very impressed with the spectacular view. It was not hard to convince the president that Yosemite Valley should be part of the national park system. In 1906, Congress passed a bill that Roosevelt then signed, transferring Yosemite Valley and the Mariposa Grove to federal control. In 1964 three protected wilderness areas were added adjacent to Yosemite National Park. These are the Ansel Adams Wilderness, the Hoover Wilderness, and the Emigrant Wilderness.

→ HETCH HETCHY: THE SECOND YOSEMITE VALLEY

Hetch Hetchy Valley on the Tuolumne River in Yosemite National Park could be called a second Yosemite Valley. It was created by the same geological forces as Yosemite Valley and has the same kind of huge granite domes and astounding waterfalls surrounding it. In 1901 the city of San Francisco had applied for permission to dam Hetch Hetchy.

When John Muir heard about this, he was outraged. "Dam Hetch Hetchy! As well dam for water-tanks the people's cathedrals and churches, for no holier temple has ever been consecrated by the heart of man,"[4] Muir cried. He wrote:

> Sad to say, this most precious and sublime feature of the Yosemite National Park, one of the greatest of

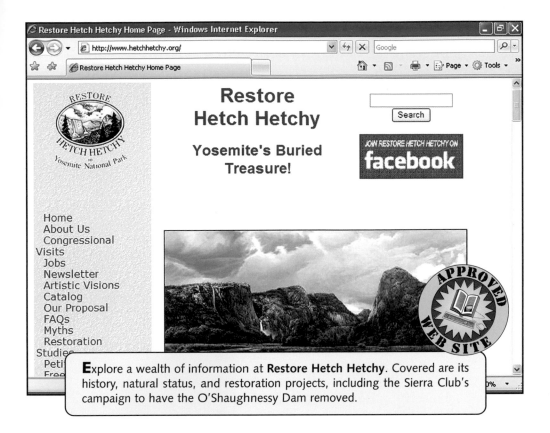

Restore Hetch Hetchy Home Page - Windows Internet Explorer

http://www.hetchhetchy.org/

Google

Restore Hetch Hetchy Home Page

Page ▾ Tools ▾

Restore Hetch Hetchy

Yosemite's Buried Treasure!

Search

JOIN RESTORE HETCH HETCHY ON
facebook

Home
About Us
Congressional Visits
Jobs
Newsletter
Artistic Visions
Catalog
Our Proposal
FAQs
Myths
Restoration Studies
Peti...
Free...

Explore a wealth of information at **Restore Hetch Hetchy**. Covered are its history, natural status, and restoration projects, including the Sierra Club's campaign to have the O'Shaughnessy Dam removed.

all our natural resources for the uplifting joy and peace and health of the people, is in danger of being dammed and made into a reservoir to help supply San Francisco with water and light, thus flooding it from wall to wall and burying its gardens and groves one or two hundred feet deep. This grossly destructive commercial scheme has long been planned and urged (though water as pure and abundant can be got from sources outside of the people's park, in a dozen different places), because of the comparative cheapness of the dam and of the territory which it is sought to divert from the great uses to which it was dedicated in the Act of 1890 establishing the Yosemite National Park.[5]

John Muir and others fought a long battle to prevent the dam from being built. But in 1908 the water rights were granted to the city of San Francisco. In 1913 the U.S. Congress passed the Raker Act. This law allowed San Francisco to construct the O'Shaughnessy Dam in the Hetch Hetchy Valley. Muir was heartbroken. He died the following year. The dam was completed in 1923, flooding the beautiful valley. In 1938 the dam was raised another 85 feet (26 meters), raising the water level of Hetch Hetchy Reservoir. San Francisco still receives some of its water supply from this reservoir.

In recent years, some environmentalists have been arguing for the removal of O'Shaughnessy Dam and the restoration of Hetch Hetchy.

The O'Shaughnessy Dam remains a ▶ controversial dam in the Tuolomne River. Many dislike the dam because of its impact on the habitats of the area, but the dam currently provides drinking water to homes in California.

➡ THE AUTOMOBILE COMES TO YOSEMITE

As time went on, Yosemite National Park attracted ever increasing numbers of visitors. To keep up with them, new trails were built and old ones were improved. New lodges and camps were

built. In 1907 the Yosemite Valley Railroad began service between Merced and El Portal. This shortened the stagecoach ride to 10 miles (16 kilometers). But the biggest advance in making Yosemite more accessible came with the advent of the automobile.

On June 23, 1900, the first automobile arrived in Yosemite Valley. Oliver Lippincott drove his Locomobile from Raymond to Wawona, and from there to Yosemite Valley. The trip took about eight hours. About a month later, Arthur and Frank Holmes drove their Stanley Steamer to Yosemite Valley all the way from San Jose. Due to the dangers of stages and autos sharing the roads, autos were banned from the park until April 1913. In the following years, more pioneers of the road would drive into Yosemite Valley.

John Muir welcomed the use of the automobile in Yosemite. He wrote:

> The principal objection urged against the puffing machines was that on the steep Yosemite grades they would cause serious accidents. The machine men roared in reply that far fewer park-going people would be killed or wounded by the auto way than by the old pre-historic wagon way. All signs indicate automobile victory, and doubtless, under certain precautionary restrictions, these useful, progressive, blunt-nosed mechanical beetles will hereafter be allowed to puff their way into all the parks and mingle their gas-breath with the breath

of the pines and waterfalls, and, from the mountaineer's standpoint, with but little harm or good. . . . Good walkers can go anywhere in these hospitable mountains without artificial ways. But most visitors have to be rolled on wheels with blankets and kitchen arrangements.[6]

In 1916 the newly created National Park Service (NPS) took over the management of Yosemite from the U.S. Army. To keep up with the growing numbers of motor vehicles entering Yosemite each year, the National Park Service began building paved roads. On July 31, 1926, Highway 140, the "All-Year Highway" from Merced to Yosemite Valley was completed. Hundreds of motorists eagerly drove the new route. The following year, 137,296

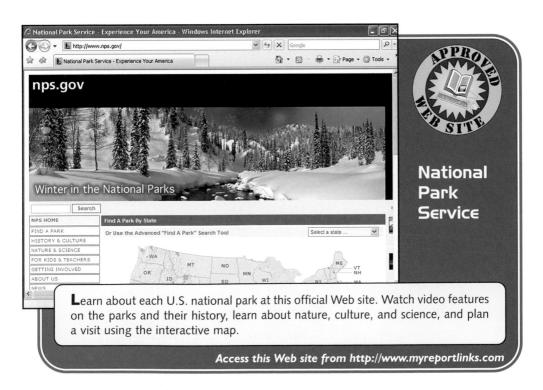

Learn about each U.S. national park at this official Web site. Watch video features on the parks and their history, learn about nature, culture, and science, and plan a visit using the interactive map.

Access this Web site from http://www.myreportlinks.com

cars entered Yosemite. The All-Year Highway resulted in the end of the once popular Yosemite Valley Railroad. The railroad stopped running in 1945.

In spite of occasional heavy traffic on park roads during the summer months, you can still enjoy the wonderful scenery while driving through Yosemite. Or, even better, you can park your car and take the free shuttles that loop around the valley floor, getting on and off at whatever stops you choose. Along the loop consisting of Northside Drive and Southside Drive in Yosemite Valley, you will see the valley's best known features—the granite domes, cliffs, and waterfalls. The valley's spectacular waterfalls, fed by the melting snow, are best seen in the months of April, May, and June. By late summer, most of the falls either slow to a trickle or dry up completely.

The Wawona Road runs south from Yosemite Valley to Wawona and the Mariposa Grove. From Tunnel View, you can see dense woods, meadows, Bridalveil Fall, and the valley's great granite walls. The drive to Hetch Hetchy Reservoir climbs the cliffs above the Tuolumne River. The Glacier Point Road climbs to Glacier Point, with its famous viewpoint high above Yosemite Valley.

The Tioga Pass Road, now a part of Highway 120, crosses the High Sierra over Tioga Pass. The

Old Tioga Road was originally built as a mining road in 1882–83. It was modernized in 1961. The road slowly climbs through pine forests, past meadows, lakes, and granite domes and spires. Just beyond Tenaya Lake, you arrive at Tuolomne Meadows. At an elevation of 8,575 feet (2,614 meters) above sea level, Tuolumne Meadows is the largest subalpine meadow in the Sierra Nevada. The Tioga Pass Road then climbs over Tioga Pass at an elevation of 9,945 feet (3,031 meters). Tioga Pass is the highest mountain pass through which you can drive in California. Because of the high altitude, Tioga Pass Road is closed due to snow usually from mid-November to mid-May.

⊜ WATERFALLS AND A "FIREFALL"

Among the features drawing visitors to Yosemite are the valley's beautiful waterfalls. Nowhere else in the world is there a collection of so many spectacular waterfalls so close together in one area. The area's numerous sheer drops and hanging valleys provide many places for waterfalls to exist.

The hanging valleys in Yosemite were created when the last glacier retreated. While a massive glacier was carving out Yosemite Valley, smaller alpine glaciers flowed downward off the upper slopes and ridges of the mountains. The smaller alpine glaciers carved smaller valleys and then

This photograph shows both the higher and lower Yosemite Falls. There are many lovely waterfalls within Yosemite.

joined the deeper valley glacier. When the ice finally retreated, the smaller valleys were left "hanging" above the main valley. In Yosemite Valley, Bridalveil Fall and Yosemite Falls flow over the edges of hanging valleys.

The main waterfalls in Yosemite Valley include Yosemite Falls, Sentinel Fall, Ribbon Fall, Staircase Fall, Royal Arch Cascade, Silver Strand Fall, El Capitan Fall, Horsetail Fall, Lehamite Fall, Bridalveil Fall, The Cascades, Nevada Fall, Illilouette Fall, and Vernal Fall. Many of the falls are ephemeral, seen only in early spring.

As if the waterfalls were not enough, tourists in Yosemite Valley during the years 1872 to 1968 were treated to the spectacle of a "firefall." In 1872, an entrepreneur named James McCauley, and trail builder Jim Conway, built a 4-mile (6.4-kilometer) toll trail to Glacier Point. One evening, McCauley pushed the embers from his campfire at Glacier Point over the edge of the cliff. Tourists down below in Yosemite Valley saw what appeared to be a glowing waterfall of sparks. They were so delighted that they asked McCauley to do it again. McCauley's sons turned the firefall into a business. Whenever enough tourists had gathered in the valley, the McCauleys charged each person $1.50. The brothers then went up the trail and built a large fire using the bark from red

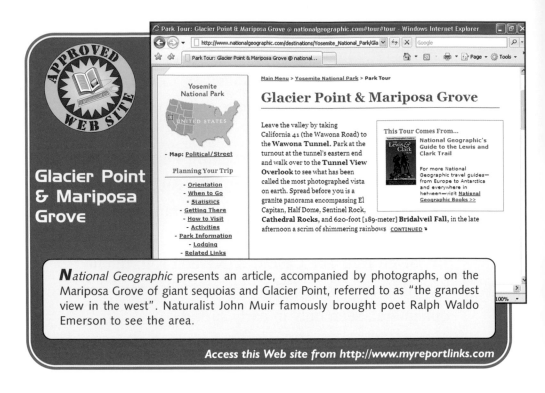

Park Tour: Glacier Point & Mariposa Grove @ nationalgeographic.com/tour#tour - Windows Internet Explorer

http://www.nationalgeographic.com/destinations/Yosemite_National_Park/Gla   Google

Park Tour: Glacier Point & Mariposa Grove @ national...   Page ▾   Tools ▾

Yosemite National Park

Main Menu > Yosemite National Park > Park Tour

Glacier Point & Mariposa Grove

- Map: Political/Street

Planning Your Trip

- Orientation
- When to Go
- Statistics
- Getting There
- How to Visit
- Activities
- Park Information
- Lodging
- Related Links

Leave the valley by taking California 41 (the Wawona Road) to the **Wawona Tunnel.** Park at the turnout at the tunnel's eastern end and walk over to the **Tunnel View Overlook** to see what has been called the most photographed vista on earth. Spread before you is a granite panorama encompassing El Capitan, Half Dome, Sentinel Rock, **Cathedral Rocks,** and 620-foot [189-meter] **Bridalveil Fall,** in the late afternoon a scrim of shimmering rainbows CONTINUED ›

This Tour Comes From...

National Geographic's Guide to the Lewis and Clark Trail

For more National Geographic travel guides— from Europe to Antarctica and everywhere in between—visit National Geographic Books >>

100%

Glacier Point & Mariposa Grove

National Geographic presents an article, accompanied by photographs, on the Mariposa Grove of giant sequoias and Glacier Point, referred to as "the grandest view in the west". Naturalist John Muir famously brought poet Ralph Waldo Emerson to see the area.

Access this Web site from http://www.myreportlinks.com

fir trees. Just after nightfall, they pushed the embers over the cliff.

The McCauleys left Yosemite in 1897. Two years later, David Curry opened Camp Curry in Yosemite Valley. He continued to build fires at Glacier Point and throw the embers over the cliff. The firefall at Glacier Point became a tradition that lasted for many years. Although the firefall remained popular with tourists, the National Park Service put a stop to it in 1968. Red fir bark was fast disappearing, and the valley's meadows were being trampled and destroyed. As park managers moved to emphasize the more natural wilderness qualities of the park, the firefall was viewed as unnatural and inappropriate in a wild setting.

➡ THE AHWAHNEE HOTEL

As tourism in Yosemite National Park grew by leaps and bounds, over the years various kinds of accommodations sprouted up to cater to the visitors. There were lodges, cabins, hotels, cottages, and campgrounds. Stephen Mather, the National Park Service director, decided that what Yosemite needed was a hotel for the most affluent visitors.

In July 1925, architect Gilbert Stanley Underwood was chosen to design the hotel. Over 5,000 tons (5,080 metric tons) of stone, 1,000 tons (1,016 metric tons) of steel, and 30,000 feet (9,144 meters) of timber had to be trucked in over treacherous mountain roads. Many earlier hotels in Yosemite had been destroyed by fire. To avoid a similar fate, the wood-like façade of the new hotel was actually made of concrete poured into rough-hewn wooden forms and stained to look like redwood.

By far the most luxurious hotel in Yosemite, the Ahwahnee, was completed in 1927. It features giant stone fireplaces, massive hand-stenciled beams, rich tapestries, American Indian artwork, landscape paintings, and elegant stained glass. The dining room has floor-to-ceiling windows and a 34-foot- (10.4-meter-) high ceiling. The Great

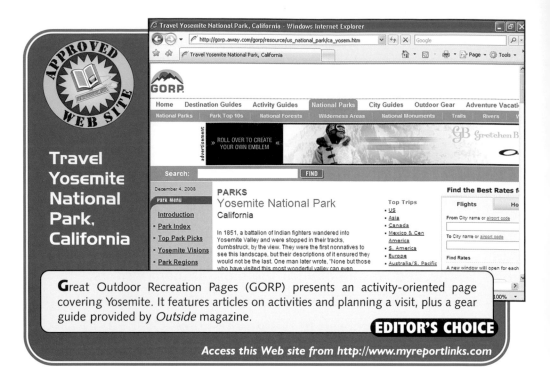

Travel Yosemite National Park, California

Great Outdoor Recreation Pages (GORP) presents an activity-oriented page covering Yosemite. It features articles on activities and planning a visit, plus a gear guide provided by *Outside* magazine.

EDITOR'S CHOICE

Access this Web site from http://www.myreportlinks.com

Lounge has ten floor-to-ceiling windows topped with original, hand-stained glass panels. Wrought-iron chandeliers hang from the ceiling.

The guest rooms tend to be small. But the gorgeous views from the windows more than make up for the dimensions of the rooms. One side of the hotel faces Glacier Point and Half Dome. The other side faces Yosemite Falls.

During World War II, the Ahwahnee served as a naval hospital from 1943 to 1945. Tourism was slow during the war years. But Yosemite was filled with military personnel. After the war was over, visitors returned in greater numbers than ever. The Ahwahnee is rather expensive, but the list of former guests includes Queen Elizabeth, Winston Churchill, John F. Kennedy, and Ronald Reagan. The Ahwahnee Hotel is now a National Historic Landmark.

During the second half of the twentieth century, the National Park Service struggled to preserve Yosemite's natural environment. Planning was needed to cope with the rapid growth in the numbers of annual visitors to the park.

Chapter

4

A mule deer in Yosemite National Park.

Yosemite Plants and Animals

Because Yosemite National Park spans such a wide range of elevations, the park's ecosystem supports a wide variety of plants and wildlife. There are more than 1,300 species of flowering plants, 223 kinds of birds, and 77 kinds of animals.

The types of vegetation in any given area depend on the specifics of the types of soil, topography, and especially the local climate, including temperatures and the amount of sunlight. And the climate varies with elevation. The higher you go in Yosemite, the cooler it gets. Elevations within Yosemite range from 1,800 feet (549 meters) at El Portal on the western boundary of the park to over 13,000 feet (3,962 meters) at the top of the tallest peaks. Each

79

zone offers habitat to a different group of plants and animals.

➔YOSEMITE'S CLIMATE

Meteorologists classify the climate in Yosemite National Park as Mediterranean. This means that the winters are generally mild, while the summers are long and hot. Daytime temperatures are usually in the 80s or 90s Fahrenheit (27 to 37 Celsius) on the floor of Yosemite Valley during the summer. And temperatures of 100°F (38°C) are not uncommon. At night the temperatures usually drop to the 50s (around 14°C). In the high country, summer temperatures rarely rise above 75°F (24°C). And it can snow there at any time of year, even during July.

Winter daytime temperatures in Yosemite Valley average from the 30s to the 50s. At night, the temperature usually falls below 30°F (⁻1°C). In the high country, winter weather is much colder. At the tops of the mountains, temperatures can drop to ⁻30°F (⁻34°C).

Most of Yosemite Valley's average annual precipitation of 36 inches (91.4 centimeters) falls between October and April. It snows from time to time. But heavy snowfalls (more than one or two feet) are rare. Much of the winter precipitation is rain. In the high country, the average annual precipitation is about 50 inches (127 centimeters). Winter brings heavy snow, closing some park

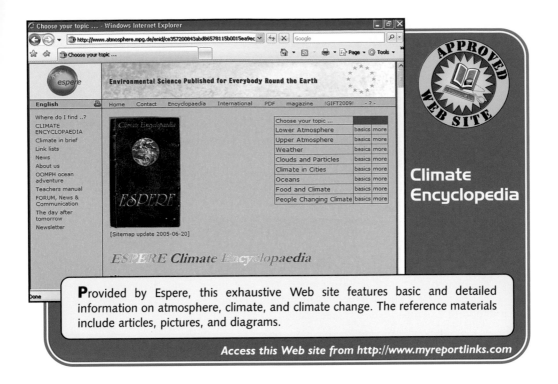

Provided by Espere, this exhaustive Web site features basic and detailed information on atmosphere, climate, and climate change. The reference materials include articles, pictures, and diagrams.

Access this Web site from http://www.myreportlinks.com

roads from late October until early June. The Tioga Pass Road is often buried beneath more than 10 feet (3 meters) of snow.

Because summer is basically a dry season, Yosemite's vegetation is dry. The small amount of summer precipitation in Yosemite comes in the form of infrequent afternoon thundershowers, especially in the high country. The thunderstorms sometimes result in forest fires caused by lightning.

YOSEMITE'S VEGETATION ZONES

Scientists have classified Yosemite into five major vegetation zones. At the lowest elevation is the foothill woodland zone. Moving higher, you come

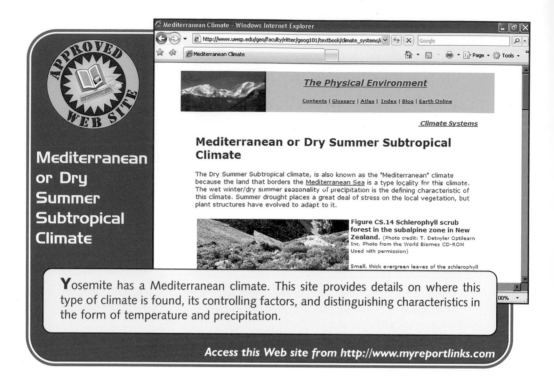

Mediterranean or Dry Summer Subtropical Climate

Mediterranean Climate - Windows Internet Explorer

http://www.uwsp.edu/geo/faculty/ritter/geog101/textbook/climate_systems/i

Google

Mediterranean Climate

Page ▾ Tools ▾

The Physical Environment

Contents | Glossary | Atlas | Index | Blog | Earth Online

Climate Systems

Mediterranean or Dry Summer Subtropical Climate

The Dry Summer Subtropical climate, is also known as the "Mediterranean" climate because the land that borders the Mediterranean Sea is a type locality for this climate. The wet winter/dry summer seasonality of precipitation is the defining characteristic of this climate. Summer drought places a great deal of stress on the local vegetation, but plant structures have evolved to adapt to it.

Figure CS.14 Schlerophyll scrub forest in the subalpine zone in New Zealand. (Photo credit: T. Detwyler Optilearn Inc. Photo from the World Biomes CD-ROM Used with permission)

Small, thick evergreen leaves of the schlerophyll

Yosemite has a Mediterranean climate. This site provides details on where this type of climate is found, its controlling factors, and distinguishing characteristics in the form of temperature and precipitation.

Access this Web site from http://www.myreportlinks.com

to the lower montane forest. Next comes the upper montane forest. Still climbing, you reach the subalpine forest, and then at the highest elevations, the alpine zone.

The foothill woodland zone is on Yosemite's western boundary. El Portal is located here, just outside the park. It is at an elevation of 1,800 feet (549 meters). This zone rises to an elevation of about 3,500 feet (1,067 meters). This area gets very little snow in winter, and summers are very hot and dry. The California poppy, the state flower also known as the golden poppy, covers fields and rolling hills in the springtime with a golden-orange carpet.

Trees in the foothill woodland zone include the blue oak, interior live oak, and gray pine. Hillsides are covered with a common type of shrub community known as chaparral. Most of the plants are small evergreen shrubs and bushes, usually less than 10 feet (3 meters) high. They tend to have small, thick, waxy leaves designed to retain moisture. They can survive long periods with no rain and recover easily after fire.

The most common chaparral plants include ceanothus, chamise, and manzanita, a shrub with distinctive smooth, reddish bark. John Muir was fascinated by the manzanita's ability to survive. "No need have they to fear the wind, so low they are and steadfastly rooted," he wrote. "Even the fires that sweep the woods seldom destroy them utterly, for they rise again from the root, and some of the dry ridges they grow on are seldom touched by fire. I must try to know them better."[1]

The lower montane forest zone extends from about 3,500 feet (1,067 meters) up to 6,000 feet (1,829 meters). It is near the western and southern boundaries of the park. Yosemite Valley and Hetch Hetchy Valley are located in this zone, as is Wawona and portions of the Mariposa Grove. Summers are still hot and dry. But winter snow can stay on the ground for several months, especially in the higher areas.

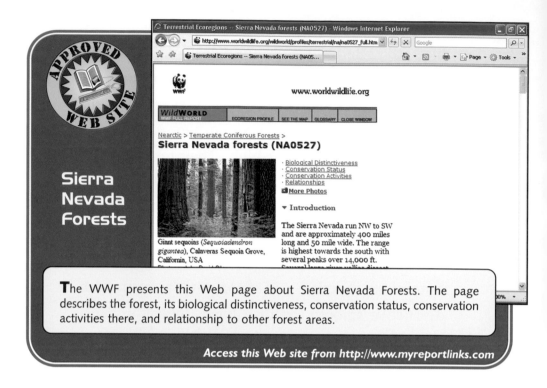

The WWF presents this Web page about Sierra Nevada Forests. The page describes the forest, its biological distinctiveness, conservation status, conservation activities there, and relationship to other forest areas.

Access this Web site from http://www.myreportlinks.com

Mixed conifer forests fill the valleys in this zone. These forests include the ponderosa pine, incense-cedar, white fir, sugar pine, giant sequoia, and Douglas fir. The Douglas fir is the most important lumber tree in the United States. But in Yosemite, the Douglas fir is protected from logging. The sugar pine is the tallest pine tree, often reaching nearly 200 feet (61 meters) in height.

Within the lower montane forest are Yosemite's three giant sequoia groves. The sequoia is the largest living thing on earth. John Muir, ever an admirer of these forest giants, wrote, "On coming in sight of them for the first time, you are likely to say, 'Oh, see what beautiful, noble-looking trees are towering there among the firs and pines!'—their grandeur being in the mean time in great part invisible, but to the living eye it will be manifested sooner or later, stealing slowly on the senses, like the grandeur of Niagara, or the lofty Yosemite domes."[2]

J. Smeaton Chase, another early wanderer in Yosemite, was equally in awe of the giant sequoias. He wrote, "The massiveness of the trunk is relieved also by a fluting of the bark which is often so regular as to be remarkable, and which adds to the architectural suggestion. This fluting is often broken up near the base of the tree into a network of tracery, the bark running into a maze of niches and foliations that is richly Gothic and beautiful. As one stands in the dream-like silence of these groves of ancient trees, the solemnity of their enormous age and size, together with the grace and fancifulness of this carved and fretted ornamentation, combine to produce a cathedral mood of quietude and receptiveness."[3]

Deciduous trees of the lower montane forest include the black oak and the western dogwood, with its beautiful white blossoms in the spring. The black oaks in Yosemite Valley once provided acorns for the valley's American Indian inhabitants. The National Park Service is working to restore black oaks to the valley.

▲ Sprouting from the Mariposa Grove, this sequoia is known as the Grizzly Giant.

The upper montane forest extends from about 6,000 feet (1,829 meters) to about 8,000 feet (2,438 meters). This zone has short, moist, cool summers and cold, wet winters. Snow cover, often as deep as six feet (1.8 meters), can remain on the ground until June. In the summer, beautiful wildflowers bloom in the meadows. These include the Jeffrey shooting star, Indian paintbrush, lupine, and Sierra primrose. Forests of this zone include red fir, lodgepole pine, Jeffrey pine, and western juniper. The red fir provided the wood and bark for the famous firefall at Glacier Point. The bark of the Jeffrey pine has a unique scent suggestive of vanilla or butterscotch.

The subalpine forest begins at around 8,000 feet (2,438 meters) and rises to about 9,500 feet (2,896 meters). This zone is characterized by long, cold, snowy winters and a short growing season. Heavy winter snows can accumulate to a depth of nine feet (2.74 meters). The subalpine forest consists of the western white pine, mountain hemlock, and lodgepole pine.

The alpine zone begins at about 9,500 feet (2,896 meters). The climate is harsh, with a very short frost-free summer and a long, cold winter with very heavy snow. This zone is above the timberline, as trees cannot survive the extreme climate. Plants in the alpine zone are very small. Among them are flowers such as penstemon, dwarf phlox and cassiope. The sky pilot is found only on summits above 11,000 feet (3,353 meters). John Muir even came across wild bees and butterflies feeding on flowers at a height of 13,000 feet (3,962 meters) above the sea.

YOSEMITE WILDLIFE

The black bear is the largest mammal in Yosemite. Black bears can weigh up to 400 pounds (181 kilograms) and can run up to 30 miles (48 kilometers) per hour. Interestingly, black bears are not always black, but can be brown, cinnamon-colored, and on rare occasions blond. They sometimes have a white patch on their chests. The black bear's diet consists of berries, fruits, insects, fish, small mammals, and even the inner layer of tree bark. In addition to their natural diet, black bears have gotten used to stealing food from humans. Black bears are omnivores so they can, and will, eat just about anything. After many years of being fed by humans, black bears have lost some of their natural fear of us. Sadly, two or three bears have to be euthanized each year because they have gotten too aggressive.

Sierra bighorn sheep inhabit the mountains at elevations above 10,000 feet (3,048 meters). They are listed as an endangered species by the federal government. Until 1986, when bighorns were reintroduced into Yosemite's high country, the last bighorn was seen in the area in 1914.

American Black Bear is part of the Smithsonian Museum of Natural History's Guide to North American Mammals. This page features in-depth information about the black bear.

John Muir was much impressed at the mountaineering abilities of bighorns. He wrote, "The wild sheep ranks highest among the animal mountaineers of the Sierra. Possessed of keen sight and scent, and strong limbs, he dwells secure amid the loftiest summits, leaping unscathed from crag to crag, up and down the fronts of giddy precipices, crossing foaming torrents and slopes of frozen snow, exposed to the wildest storms, yet maintaining a brave, warm life, and developing from generation to generation in perfect strength and beauty."[4]

University of Michigan Museum of Zoology

Animal Diversity Web

About Us ❖ Special Topics ✦ Teaching ❖ About Animal Names ✦ Help

Featuring

black skimmer
Rynchops niger

Browse Kingdom Animalia:

Amphibians	Insects
Arthropods	Mammals
Birds	Mollusks
Bony Fishes	Reptiles
Echinoderms	Sharks
and others	

Search

Animal Diversity Web

Because of its diversity, Yosemite is home to many animal species. At this site you can read about many species' names, classification, range, habitat, life, behavior, and conservation efforts.

Access this Web site from http://www.myreportlinks.com

Other large mammals in Yosemite include the mule deer, the mountain lion, and the coyote. The mule deer is one of the largest American deer and can weigh up to 450 pounds (204 kilograms). The mountain lion is the largest cat in North America. It can weigh up to 250 pounds (113 kilograms). Mountain lions are reclusive creatures, and your chances of seeing one in Yosemite are slim. Coyotes on the other hand are quite common. They are unafraid of humans and can often be seen near the roads in Yosemite.

Yosemite's small mammals include bobcats, raccoons, porcupines, yellow-bellied marmots, chipmunks, squirrels, and more. The pika lives at elevations above 8,000 feet (2,438 meters). It is a small relative of the rabbit, and is often seen on rocky hillsides.

Yosemite is home to more than three hundred bird species. Most common among these are the raven, Steller's jay, mountain chickadee, Clark's nutcracker, gray-crowned rosy finch, American dipper, blue grouse, great horned owl, great gray owl, California spotted owl, peregrine falcon, and a variety of woodpeckers. The Steller's jay is a bold and noisy bird that will eagerly steal your food if given the chance. The tiny calliope hummingbird and Anna's hummingbird can often be seen in flower-filled mountain meadows. These tiny birds are fueled by a sugar-rich diet equivalent to a human eating 155,000 calories a day.

Amphibians and reptiles in Yosemite include various kinds of frogs and toads, lizards, and snakes. The Mt. Lyell salamander inhabits Yosemite's granite domes and talus slopes from 4,000 to 12,000 feet (1,219 to 3,658 meters) in elevation. It uses its toes and strong tail to climb sheer cliffs and boulders in search of food.

Five species of trout inhabit Yosemite's lakes and streams. But only one of these, the rainbow trout, is native to the area. The other four were introduced through fish-planting programs in the late 1800s and early 1900s. Today about fifty lakes in the park have self-sustaining populations

Anna's hummingbird is one of more than three hundred bird species found in Yosemite.

of nonnative trout. Studies have shown that these fish are eating the eggs and tadpoles of native frogs, which are quickly becoming extinct. Efforts are underway to remove these nonnative fish and return the lakes to their natural state.

Among Yosemite's insects are wild bees and several kinds of beautiful butterflies. These include the Western tiger swallowtail, the Monarch, and the stunning iridescent blue pipevine swallowtail.

Chapter

5

Yosemite National Park can be enjoyed at any time of the year. Efforts have been undertaken to ensure it stays that way.

Protecting Yosemite's Environment

In 1984, the United Nations Educational, Scientific, and Cultural Organization (UNESCO) named Yosemite National Park as a World Heritage Site. This means that UNESCO recognized the value to humanity of preserving Yosemite. Conservationists today are aware of the dangers to Yosemite's environment. Indeed, the struggle to preserve Yosemite and its treasure trove of scenic wonders began even before it became a national park.

During the late 1800s, grazing sheep turned Yosemite's lush meadows into choking dustbowls. John Muir became concerned over sheep ranching and logging practices, especially the cutting down of giant sequoias. Muir wrote:

Running fires are set everywhere, with a view to clearing the ground of prostrate trunks, to facilitate the movements of the flocks and improve the pastures. The entire forest belt is thus swept and devastated from one extremity of the range to the other, and, with the exception of the resinous *Pinus contorta*, Sequoia suffers most of all. Indians burn off the underbrush in certain localities to facilitate deer-hunting, mountaineers and lumbermen carelessly allow their camp-fires to run; but the fires of the sheepmen, or muttoneers, form more than ninety per cent. of all destructive fires that range the Sierra forests.[1]

It was through the strenuous efforts of Galen Clark, John Muir, and others that Yosemite was established as a national park in the first place.

⊜ LOVING YOSEMITE

The phenomenal growth in tourism and recreation has had an impact on Yosemite's landscape. Smog drifting eastward from California's Central Valley has also affected the vistas and the health of some of the vegetation in the park.

During World War II, tourism in Yosemite National Park had slowed dramatically. Only about forty thousand people a year ventured into Yosemite. But once the war was over, it was off to the races. In 1946 about 750,000 tourists visited Yosemite. By 1966 the park had 2 million visitors a year. By 1970 the scene in Yosemite Valley had become almost urbanized.

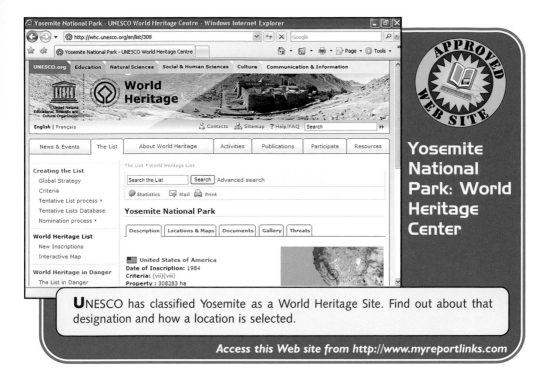

UNESCO has classified Yosemite as a World Heritage Site. Find out about that designation and how a location is selected.

Access this Web site from http://www.myreportlinks.com

The National Park Service came up with a plan that included a free shuttle-bus system to carry visitors around the valley. Meanwhile, hiking trails into the backcountry had also become congested. This was especially true in popular places such as the lakes off the Tioga Pass Road. Beginning in 1972, a wilderness permit was required for hikers. A quota system set limits to certain popular backcountry sites to ensure a true wilderness experience for all visitors.

The number of visitors to Yosemite stabilized at about 2 million people a year during the 1970s. However, this would prove to be just a temporary pause. By 1980 a million automobiles a year were

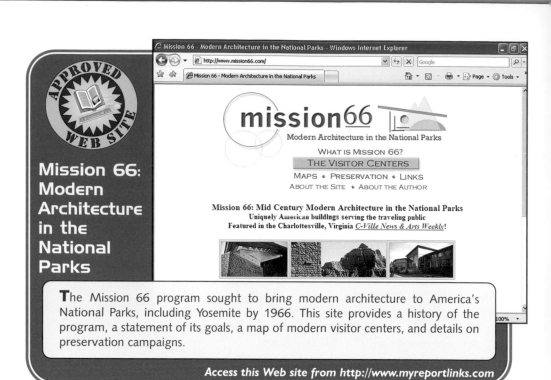

Mission 66:
Modern
Architecture
in the
National
Parks

mission66

Modern Architecture in the National Parks

WHAT IS MISSION 66?

THE VISITOR CENTERS

MAPS • PRESERVATION • LINKS

ABOUT THE SITE • ABOUT THE AUTHOR

Mission 66: Mid Century Modern Architecture in the National Parks
Uniquely American buildings serving the traveling public
Featured in the Charlottesville, Virginia *C-Ville News & Arts Weekly*!

The Mission 66 program sought to bring modern architecture to America's National Parks, including Yosemite by 1966. This site provides a history of the program, a statement of its goals, a map of modern visitor centers, and details on preservation campaigns.

Access this Web site from http://www.myreportlinks.com

entering the park. The National Park Service was determined to come up with a new plan.

⟶ THE GENERAL MANAGEMENT PLAN (GMP) OF 1980

In 1980, Yosemite National Park created a General Management Plan (GMP). That year the number of visitors reached 2.5 million. The NPS needed to gain control over the pace of development in Yosemite Valley. At the time, there were more than one thousand buildings on the floor of the valley. These included homes, apartments, lodgings, garages, stores, and restaurants. Cars, trucks, and buses used the thirty miles of road in the valley.

The main purpose of the 1980 General Management Plan was to find a way to balance the preservation and protection of Yosemite's natural beauty with the needs of visitors. To achieve this result, the plan listed the following five goals: reclaim the park's priceless natural beauty, markedly reduce traffic congestion, allow natural processes to prevail, reduce crowding, and promote visitor understanding and enjoyment.

From the beginning, the plan generated a great deal of controversy. It called for reducing traffic congestion by putting restrictions on private cars and increasing public transportation. Ultimately, the planners proposed removing all parking lots and private vehicles from Yosemite Valley and the Mariposa Grove. Shuttle buses would carry visitors into Yosemite Valley and the Mariposa Grove from parking lots outside the park. These proposals provoked a largely negative response from the public. There were also objections to a proposal to establish visitor-use levels for different sights.

The planners also proposed relocating most of Yosemite Valley's commercial services to locations outside the park. Other proposals called for changes in the campgrounds. For the most part, the 1980 General Management Plan listed worthy goals and a roadmap for how to get there. But the 1980s were a time of diminishing funds for national parks. And in the face of heated public

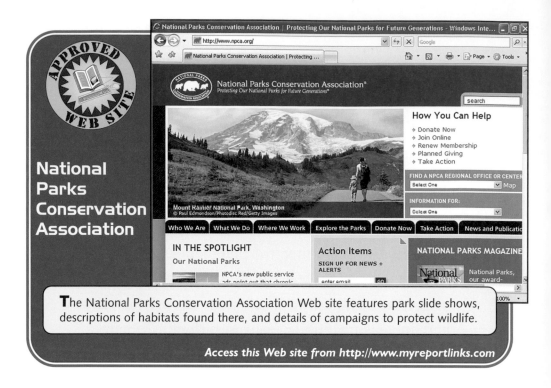

The National Parks Conservation Association Web site features park slide shows, descriptions of habitats found there, and details of campaigns to protect wildlife.

Access this Web site from http://www.myreportlinks.com

opposition, there was a lack of will on the part of various government agencies to take action. So there was very little progress toward meeting the goals of the 1980 General Management Plan.

Meanwhile, congestion in Yosemite Valley continued to worsen. In 1996, Yosemite had 4.2 million visitors, the highest number ever. Then in 1997, Mother Nature intervened.

➔ FORCES OF NATURE

Yosemite Valley has had a long history of natural events shaping the landscape. These included devastating rock slides and occasional earthquakes. There have also been massive floods, such as in

1937 and 1955. But during the first few days of January 1997, the biggest flood in Yosemite's recorded history occurred. Unseasonably warm weather combined with heavy rain, even above the 9,000-foot (2,743-meter) level, caused snow to melt. The Merced River, clogged with trees, brush, and boulders, overflowed its banks. Floodwaters in the valley reached as high as 10 feet (3 meters) in places.

Many structures in Yosemite Valley were destroyed. These included employee housing and cabins at Yosemite Lodge. Campgrounds were also destroyed. The rampaging floodwaters picked up picnic tables and fire grills and dropped them off in new locations. The sewer system was destroyed. The park was mostly evacuated, except for employees who worked on the cleanup. Yosemite remained closed to visitors for more than two months.

In a sense, the devastating flood of 1997 proved to be a blessing in disguise. The National Park Service now had an opportunity to make some of the changes that had been proposed in the 1980 General Management Plan. Expensive damage to some structures ensured that they would not be rebuilt. The total number of campgrounds in the valley was cut in half. And locations of campgrounds were changed. Campgrounds would no longer be situated in the floodplain of the Merced River. Also,

NATIONAL PARK FOUNDATION
The National Charitable Partner of America's National Parks

Who We Help | Who Helps Us | Discover Parks | Get Involved | About NPF | News | Search

century of giving

View our interactive timeline and see some of what's been happening in park philanthropy over the last 100 years ●

SUPPOR
We need
protect A
Make A
Learn ho

STAY CO
GoParks
Sign Up

CELEBRATE THE HOLIDAYS
The Lighting of the

Who We Help
The mission of the National

EXPLORI
For mor
private
helping

00%

Learn how the National Park Foundation helps America's National Parks. Its Web site describes its partnerships and campaigns. The site also includes feature articles from *Parks* magazine, plus photo and essay contests.

Access this Web site from http://www.myreportlinks.com

employee housing and some visitor lodging were permanently removed.

⊜ THE YOSEMITE VALLEY PLAN OF 2000

In 2000 the National Park Service prepared another plan to protect Yosemite's natural environment. The Yosemite Valley Plan is an outgrowth of the earlier 1980 General Management Plan. The new plan continues to strive for a reduction in the number of vehicles in Yosemite. One way to do this is to make fewer parking spaces available in the valley. This part of the plan has yet to accomplish its stated goal. Public opposition continues, as many people fear restrictions on private vehicles will make Yosemite less accessible.

The new plan also includes measures to preserve the wilderness environment in several ways. The plan calls for restoration of meadows and wetlands and reintroduction of prescribed burns. Ozone pollution in the air is causing tissue damage to the giant sequoia trees. This causes greater vulnerability to insect infestation and disease. Since the seeds of the sequoia require fire-cleared soil to germinate, a long history of fire suppression had reduced these trees' ability to reproduce. The new policy of setting prescribed fires has improved the germination rate.

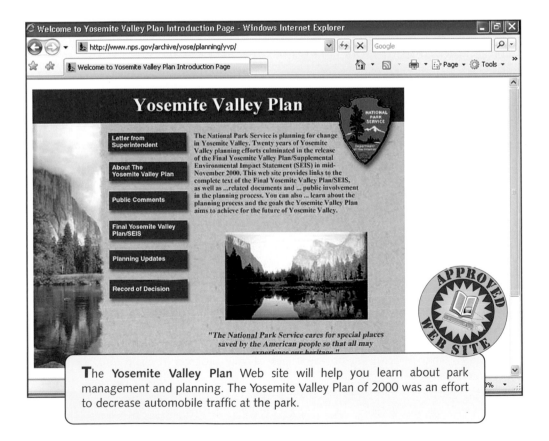

The **Yosemite Valley Plan** Web site will help you learn about park management and planning. The Yosemite Valley Plan of 2000 was an effort to decrease automobile traffic at the park.

The National Park Service has documented more than 130 nonnative plant species within Yosemite's boundaries. Some of these nonnative species aggressively invade and displace the native plant communities. This results in impacts on the park's resources. Some nonnative species may cause an increase in the fire frequency of an area. The National Park Service is actively trying to control the nonnative plant species that pose the most serious threat. These include the spotted knapweed, yellow star-thistle, bull thistle, and Himalayan blackberry.

The National Park Service is also monitoring the populations of nonnative animal species in Yosemite that threaten the park's native species.

Sign up with the WebRangers program and you can send park postcards, view webcams, and share your pictures and stories. You'll also get a virtual Ranger Station, which enables you to keep track of your progress in completing the educational activities on the site.

Access this Web site from http://www.myreportlinks.com

 **N**onnative plant species are a problem in Yosemite. At this site, the U.S. Fish and Wildlife Service describes its efforts to control them.

Access this Web site from http://www.myreportlinks.com

Native fish populations and aquatic ecosystems have been decimated by the introduction of thirty nonnative fish species within the Sierra Nevada Mountains. Yosemite has also become a habitat for nonnative species such as the wild turkey, white-tailed ptarmigan, and bullfrogs.

It will probably take many years for the goals of the Yosemite Valley Plan to be realized. Traffic congestion continues to be a problem in the valley. But the annual number of visitors has decreased from 4 million in the 1990s to the 3 million range in the first decade of the twenty-first century. The number of backpackers on Yosemite's trails also peaked during the 1990s at about fifty thousand per year. This number has also decreased slightly since then.

Chapter

6

There are many ways to enjoy the magnificence of Yosemite National Park.

Recreational Activities

Yosemite National Park is open to visitors throughout the year. The park offers something for everyone. Hiking and camping are probably the most popular activities. Many prefer the more challenging sports of rock climbing or mountain climbing. There are 1,505 campsites and 1,517 rooms and tent cabins in the park. Campers are advised to reserve a site well in advance. There are also plenty of places to stay in nearby communities or on adjacent national forest land.

Some people like to take in the scenery of Yosemite Valley's granite domes and waterfalls while riding a bicycle. There are twelve miles (19.3 kilometers) of bicycle trails in Yosemite Valley. Bicycles can be rented at Yosemite Lodge and Curry Village. If you prefer to ride a horse, three different stables in the park offer daily two-hour to full-day horseback riding trips.

Some like it hot. Summer is a good time for a variety of water sports and fishing. On hot early summer days, the Merced or Tuolumne Rivers are good places for rafting. Tenaya Lake is an especially good place for kayaking or swimming. But the water is cold— ice cold. Anglers can find five types of trout in several of Yosemite's streams and lakes.

Some like it cold. Yosemite's Badger Pass is a wonderful spot for downhill and cross-country ski-ing. There is an excellent ski school at Badger Pass. There are several fine cross-country ski trails in other parts of the park. Snowboarding and snowshoeing are gaining in popularity. Curry Vil-lage in Yosemite Valley has an open-air ice skating rink. Some visitors hang glide in the park, but the National Park Service does not encourage this.

➡ BECAUSE IT'S THERE!

When asked why he climbed Mount Everest, Edmund Hillary, the first person to do so, was reported to have replied, "Because it's there!" Perhaps that is why so many rock climbers from around the world flock to Yosemite Valley each year. Nowhere else can they find such an incredi-ble collection of 3,000-foot- (914-meter-) high granite monoliths, sheer spires, and near-vertical

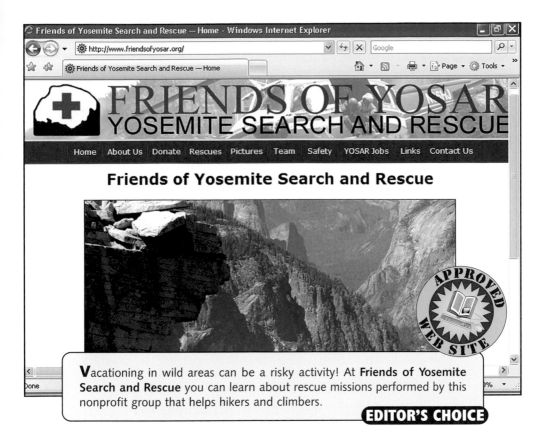

Friends of Yosemite Search and Rescue — Home - Windows Internet Explorer

http://www.friendsofyosar.org/

Friends of Yosemite Search and Rescue — Home

Page ▼ Tools ▼

FRIENDS OF YOSAR
YOSEMITE SEARCH AND RESCUE

Home | About Us | Donate | Rescues | Pictures | Team | Safety | YOSAR Jobs | Links | Contact Us

Friends of Yosemite Search and Rescue

Vacationing in wild areas can be a risky activity! At **Friends of Yosemite Search and Rescue** you can learn about rescue missions performed by this nonprofit group that helps hikers and climbers.

EDITOR'S CHOICE

APPROVED WEB SITE

walls like El Capitan and Half Dome. While many climbers love the challenge of clambering up rock walls, others prefer to hike to the tops of high Sierra peaks.

John Muir was one of the first to climb many of Yosemite's granite domes and high mountain peaks. What happened to Muir as he climbed 13,157-foot- (4,010-meter-) high Mount Ritter, in the Ansel Adams Wilderness adjacent to Yosemite, shows that mountain climbing could be very dangerous. Muir wrote:

. . . After gaining a point about halfway to the top, I was brought to a dead stop, with arms outspread, clinging close to the face of the rock, unable to move hand or foot either up or down. My doom appeared fixed. I must fall. There would be a moment of bewilderment, and then a lifeless rumble down the one general precipice to the glacier below. When this final danger flashed in upon me, I became nerve-shaken for the first time since setting foot on the mountain, and my mind seemed to fill with a stifling smoke. Then my trembling muscles became firm again, every rift and flaw in the rock was seen as through a microscope, and my limbs moved with a positiveness and precision with which I seemed to have nothing at all to do.[1]

Back in 1868, the famous geologist Josiah Whitney gazed upon Half Dome in Yosemite Valley. Convinced that nobody could possibly climb such a steep rock, he said, "Never has been, and never will be trodden by human foot."[2] In October 1875, George Anderson scaled Half Dome, building a rope ladder as he went up. Within a few weeks, several others climbed to the top of Half Dome, making use of Anderson's rope ladder. Among them were John Muir, Galen Clark, and Sally Dutcher, the first woman to climb Half Dome. Steel cables are now installed in Half Dome for use by today's rock climbers.

Rock climbing in Yosemite has become so popular that many people attempt to climb Half Dome or some other granite dome with no prior

El Capitan is a popular wall for rock climbing within Yosemite National Park.

experience. Many people are aware that practicing rock climbing techniques before venturing thousands of feet up a rock wall is a good idea. The Yosemite Mountaineering School is regarded as one of the country's best. It offers top-rate instruction in rock and mountain climbing skills. Boulders are scattered throughout Yosemite Valley. They provide a perfect place for bouldering, or practicing rock climbing moves close to the ground. Remember that you are not allowed to damage the rock.

➔FAVORITE HIKING TRAILS IN YOSEMITE

Hiking and backpacking are very popular in Yosemite. The more than 800 miles (1,287 kilometers) of trails throughout the park provide plenty of opportunity to experience a variety of scenery on foot. Backpackers can take long-distance trails into Yosemite's backcountry wilderness. Many shorter trails are excellent for day hikes or short walks. Permits are not required for hikes in Yosemite Valley. But wilderness permits are required year-round for all overnight hikes into the Yosemite backcountry. The permits are free of charge and are issued under a quota system at visitor contact stations.

Popular day hike trails that involve no climbing include the Yosemite Valley Loops and the Mirror Lake Trail and Tenaya Canyon Loop, and

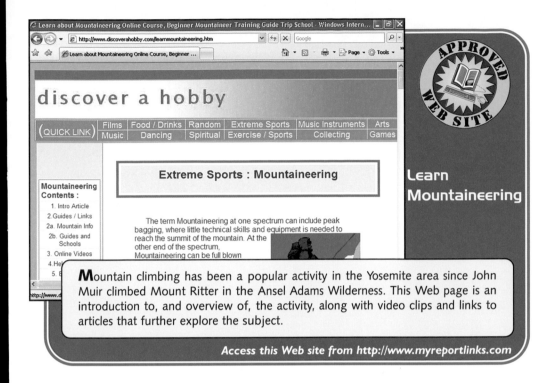

discover a hobby

	Films	Food / Drinks	Random	Extreme Sports	Music Instruments	Arts
(QUICK LINK)	Music	Dancing	Spiritual	Exercise / Sports	Collecting	Games

Extreme Sports : Mountaineering

Mountaineering
Contents :
1. Intro Article
2. Guides / Links
2a. Mountain Info
2b. Guides and
    Schools
3. Online Videos
4. He
5. B

The term Mountaineering at one spectrum can include peak
bagging, where little technical skills and equipment is needed to
reach the summit of the mountain. At the
other end of the spectrum,
Mountaineering can be full blown

**Learn
Mountaineering**

Mountain climbing has been a popular activity in the Yosemite area since John Muir climbed Mount Ritter in the Ansel Adams Wilderness. This Web page is an introduction to, and overview of, the activity, along with video clips and links to articles that further explore the subject.

Access this Web site from http://www.myreportlinks.com

the Mariposa Grove. The scenery is spectacular, and the walking is easy. Other hiking trails are considered moderate to difficult. Among the more challenging hikes are the trails to Inspiration Point, Yosemite Falls, Vernal and Nevada Falls, Half Dome, the four-mile trail to Glacier Point, and the Chilnualna Falls trail in Wawona. These are just a few of the many trails in Yosemite.

The best way to truly experience Yosemite's wilderness paradise is to shoulder a backpack and sleeping bag and head for the high country. According to writer Ann Zwinger, "I suspect the real glories of Yosemite belong to the backpackers,

Each year millions of people venture into the wilderness that is Yosemite.

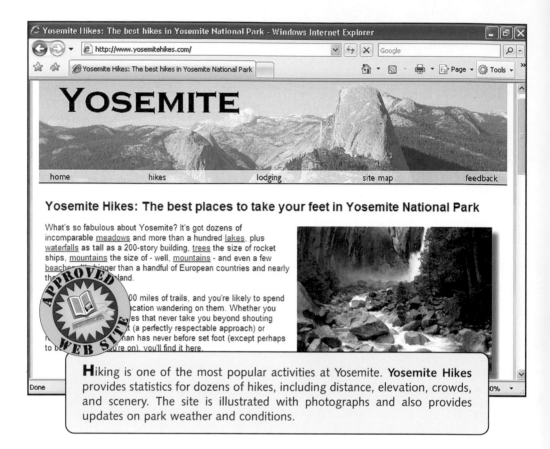

Yosemite Hikes: The best hikes in Yosemite National Park - Windows Internet Explorer

http://www.yosemitehikes.com/

Yosemite Hikes: The best hikes in Yosemite National Park

YOSEMITE

| home | hikes | lodging | site map | feedback |

Yosemite Hikes: The best places to take your feet in Yosemite National Park

What's so fabulous about Yosemite? It's got dozens of incomparable meadows and more than a hundred lakes, plus waterfalls as tall as a 200-story building, trees the size of rocket ships, mountains the size of - well, mountains - and even a few beaches. It's bigger than a handful of European countries and nearly the size of Rhode Island.

...00 miles of trails, and you're likely to spend ...cation wandering on them. Whether you ...es that never take you beyond shouting ...t (a perfectly respectable approach) or ...an has never before set foot (except perhaps to b...ou're on), you'll find it here.

Hiking is one of the most popular activities at Yosemite. **Yosemite Hikes** provides statistics for dozens of hikes, including distance, elevation, crowds, and scenery. The site is illustrated with photographs and also provides updates on park weather and conditions.

the trudgers and trekkers, those who finish a strenuous climb and wait for their psyches to catch up, suffer a thunderstorm on an alpine fell, and most of all, let the night spirits seep into their sleep. The real glories of Yosemite belong to those who are comfortable with being uncomfortable, who know it's all right to be afraid, to be cold, wet, tired, and hungry, to be euphoric and, on occasion, ecstatic."[3]

Backpackers can choose from a variety of trails that cross Yosemite's high country. One of these is the John Muir Trail, a 211-mile (340-kilometer) trail that follows the Sierra Crest between Yosemite and Sequoia National Parks. The trail begins in Yosemite Valley at Happy Isles on the Merced River. It continues over Cathedral Pass to Tuolumne Meadows. It then travels along the Lyell Fork of the Tuolumne River. The John Muir Trail then crosses Donohue Pass at an elevation of 11,065 feet (3,373 meters) on the border between Yosemite National Park and the Ansel Adams Wilderness.

More than 3 million people per year visit Yosemite. But most of them never venture into the wilderness. You can still find solitude in Yosemite. All you have to do is take a backpacking trip into Yosemite's high country. You will feel as though you are hiking in the footsteps of John Muir.

Report Links

The Internet sites described below can be accessed at
http://www.myreportlinks.com

▶**Yosemite National Park: National Park Service**
Editor's Choice The official Web site of Yosemite National Park.

▶**Visit California**
Editor's Choice Explore California by at the state tourism office's official site.

▶**Yosemite National Park**
Editor's Choice Interested in an active vacation at Yosemite? Then, check out this Web site.

▶**Friends of Yosemite Search and Rescue**
Editor's Choice This nonprofit group helps hikers and climbers who run into problems at Yosemite.

▶**The Yosemite Association**
Editor's Choice Plan a visit to Yosemite, or become a park supporter.

▶**Travel Yosemite National Park, California**
Editor's Choice See how you can get active at Yosemite National Park.

▶**American Black Bear**
All about the black bear, Yosemite's largest inhabitant.

▶**Animal Diversity Web**
Find out how the animal kingdom is classified, and study individual species.

▶**Climate Encyclopedia**
Read all about atmosphere, climate, and climate change from this online encyclopedia.

▶**Cracking the Ice Age**
Learn about the shifts in the earth's structure and composition that led to the formation of Yosemite Valley.

▶**The Geologic Story of Yosemite Valley**
Discover the history of Yosemite Valley.

▶**Glacier Point & Mariposa Grove**
Glacier Point has been referred to as "the grandest view in the west."

▶**Grizzly Bear**
Grizzly bears are an important species from Yosemite's past.

▶**John Muir Exhibit**
John Muir was a legendary naturalist, conservationist, and writer.

▶**Learn Mountaineering**
Who wants to be a mountaineer? Learn about the sport.

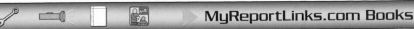
Report Links

The Internet sites described below can be accessed at
http://www.myreportlinks.com

▶**Mediterranean or Dry Summer Subtropical Climate**
Find out more about the Mediterranean climate, the type found at Yosemite.

▶**Mission 66: Modern Architecture in the National Parks**
Learn about historical efforts to bring modern architecture to America's national parks.

▶**National Park Foundation**
The National Park Foundation helps the national parks.

▶**National Parks Conservation Association**
The NPCA helps protect habitats and wildlife in America's national parks.

▶**National Park Service**
Plan a visit, or read about the history, nature, science, and culture of America's national parks.

▶**Restore Hetch Hetchy**
There are ongoing efforts to preserve Hetch Hetchy, known as the "second Yosemite Valley."

▶**Sierra Nevada Forests**
Find out why scientists value the Sierra Nevada forests.

▶**U.S. Fish & Wildlife Service's Environmental Contaminants Program**
Discover how scientists are overcoming the problem of nonnative plant species.

▶**WebRangers**
Become a virtual park ranger by participating in the WebRangers program.

▶*Yosemite: The Embattled Wilderness*
Explore the history of Yosemite from the Civil War era to the end of the twentieth century.

▶**Yosemite and the Mariposa Grove: A Preliminary Report, 1865**
Renowned landscape architect Frederick Law Olmsted had a role in developing Yosemite.

▶**Yosemite Falls**
Yosemite Falls is the tallest waterfall in North America. Browse this site about the world's waterfalls.

▶**Yosemite Hikes**
Hiking is one of the most popular activities at Yosemite.

▶**Yosemite National Park: World Heritage Center**
See how Yosemite National Park became a World Heritage Site.

▶**Yosemite Valley Plan**
Develop an understanding of park policy by reviewing the Yosemite Valley Plan of 2000.

Ahwahneechee—A Southern Sierra Miwok tribe; the first people to settle in Yosemite Valley, around 2,000 B.C.

bear box—A secure box in which food can be protected from bears.

chaparral—A common type of shrub community that grows at low elevations away from the coast in California.

climate—Weather conditions that are usual for a place.

conifer—A tree with cones.

continental plates—Interlocking pieces of land that make up the earth's continents.

deciduous—Losing leaves during the fall of each year.

environment—Surrounding conditions that influence the life of plants and animals.

erosion—The slow wearing away of the land by wind, water, and other means.

exfoliation—The process by which sheets of rock fracture and "peel off" from the surface of a formation.

geologist—A scientist who studies the origin, history, and structure of the earth.

giant sequoia—A tree; the most massive of which is the largest living thing on earth.

glacier—A large body of ice that moves down valleys under the force of gravity.

gold rush—The influx into California of many thousands of miners after gold was discovered at Sutter's Mill in January 1848.

granite—Hard rock made up of four minerals in varying amounts (quartz, feldspar, biotite, hornblende).

grizzly bear—A large North American bear, now extinct in California and Mexico.

ice age—A period of colder climate when much of North America was covered by thick glaciers.

land bridge—Land connecting Alaska and Siberia during the last ice age when the sea level was much lower.

mammal—A class of animals covered with hair (or fur or wool) that feed milk to their young.

manzanita—A shrub with distinctive smooth, reddish bark.

meteorologist—A scientist who studies climate and weather conditions, and makes weather predictions.

padres—Spanish word for priests (or fathers).

pika—A small relative of the rabbit.

reservation—A tract of public land set aside for use by American Indians.

reservoir—A place where a large amount of water is stored.

species—A group of living things that resemble one another, have common ancestors, and can breed together.

wilderness—An uninhabited and uncultivated area of land.

Chapter 1. Nature's Grandest Temple

1. Ansel Adams (photographs) and John Muir (text), Charlotte E. Mauk, ed. *Yosemite and the Sierra Nevada* (Boston: Houghton Mifflin Company, 1948), p. 11.

2. Tim Palmer (text) and William Neill (photographs), *Yosemite: The Promise of Wildness* (Yosemite National Park: The Yosemite Association, 1994), p. 15.

3. John Muir, *My First Summer in the Sierra* (Boston: Houghton Mifflin Company, 1911), p. 175.

4. Palmer and Neill, p. 21.

5. J. Smeaton Chase, *Yosemite Trails: Exploring the High Sierra* (Palo Alto, Calif.: Tioga Publishing Company, 1987), p. 3. (first published in 1911 by Houghton Mifflin, New York)

6. Ann Marie Brown, *Yosemite* (Emeryville, Calif.: Avalon Travel Publishing, Inc., 2003), p. 64.

7. Palmer and Neill, p. 20.

8. Alfred Runte, *Yosemite: The Embattled Wilderness* (Lincoln: University of Nebraska Press, 1990), p. 15.

9. Muir, *Our National Parks* (Boston: Houghton Mifflin Company, 1901), <http://www.yosemite.ca.us/john_muir_writings/our_national_parks/chapter_2.html> (February 7, 2009).

Chapter 2. History of the Yosemite Region

1. John Muir, *Our National Parks* (Madison: The University of Wisconsin Press, 1981), p. 84. (first published in 1901 by Houghton Mifflin, Boston)

2. Ibid., p. 86.

3. David Robertson, *West of Eden: A History of the Art and Literature of Yosemite* (Yosemite Natural History Association and Wilderness Press, 1984), p. 37.

4. Ted Orland, *Man & Yosemite: A Photographer's View of the Early Years* (Santa Cruz, Calif.: The Image Continuum Press, 1985), p. 19.

5. Ibid.

6. Alfred Runte, *Yosemite: The Embattled Wilderness* (Lincoln: University of Nebraska Press, 1990), p. 12.

7. Ibid.

8. Hank Johnston, *The Yosemite Grant, 1864–1906: A Pictorial History* (Yosemite, Calif.: Yosemite Association, 1995), p. 53–54.

Chapter 3. History of Yosemite National Park

1. Jeffrey P. Schaffer, *Yosemite National Park: A Complete Hiker's Guide* (Berkeley, Calif.: Wilderness Press, 2006), p. 13.

2. Ibid.

3. John McKinney, *California's National Parks: A Day Hiker's Guide* (Berkeley, Calif.: Wilderness Press, 2005), p. 6.

4. Schaffer, p. 13.

5. John Muir, *The Yosemite* (Boston, Houghton Mifflin Company, 1912), <http://www.sierraclub.org/john_muir_exhibit/frameindex.html?http://www.sierraclub.org/john_muir_exhibit/writings/the_yosemite/chapter_16.html> (February 9, 2009).

6. Shirley Sargent, *John Muir in Yosemite* (Yosemite, Calif.: Flying Spur Press, 1971), p. 43.

Chapter 4. Yosemite Plants and Animals

1. John Muir, *My First Summer in the Sierra* (Boston: Houghton Mifflin Company, 1911), p. 118.

2. Muir, *The Mountains of California* (New York: The Century Co., 1894), <http://www.gutenberg.org/files/10012/10012-8.txt> (February 9, 2009).

3. J. Smeaton Chase, *Yosemite Trails: Exploring the High Sierra* (Palo Alto, Calif.: Tioga Publishing Company, 1987), pp. 128–129. (first published in 1911 by Houghton Mifflin)

4. Ibid., p. 500.

Chapter 5. Protecting Yosemite's Environment

1. John Muir, *The Mountains of California* (New York: The Century Co., 1894), <http://www.gutenberg.org/files/10012/10012-8.txt> (February 9, 2009).

Chapter 6. Recreational Activities

1. David Robertson, *West of Eden: A History of the Art and Literature of Yosemite* (Yosemite Natural History Association and Wilderness Press, 1984), p. 41.

2. Ann Marie Brown, *Yosemite* (Emeryville, Calif.: Avalon Travel Publishing, Inc., 2003), p. 52.

3. Galen Rowell, *Yosemite & the Wild Sierra* (Seattle: Sasquatch Books, 2003), p. 27.

Adams, Ansel (photographs) and John Muir (text). *Yosemite and the Sierra Nevada*. Boston: Houghton Mifflin, 1948.

Armentrout, David and Patricia. *Historic Sites and Monuments*. Vero Beach, Fla.: Rourke Publishers, 2002.

Brown, Ann Marie. *Yosemite*. Emeryville, Calif.: Avalon Travel Publishing, Inc., 2006.

Halvorsen, Lisa. *Yosemite*. Woodbridge, Conn.: Blackbirch Press, 2000.

Hamilton, John. *Yosemite National Park*. Edina, Minn.: Abdo Publishing, 2005.

McKinney, John. *California's National Parks: A Day Hiker's Guide*. Berkeley, Calif.: Wilderness Press, 2005.

Muir, John. William Cronon, ed. *Nature Writings*. New York: Library Classics of the United States, 1997.

————— . Our National Parks. Madison: The University of Wisconsin Press, 1981.

Rowell, Galen. *Yosemite & the Wild Sierra*. Seattle: Sasquatch Books, 2003.

Schaffer, Jeffrey P. Yosemite National Park: A Complete Hiker's Guide. Berkeley, Calif.: Wilderness Press, 2006.

Warrick, Karen Clemens. *John Muir: Crusader for the Wilderness*. Berkeley Heights, N.J.: Enslow Publishers, Inc., 2002.